JANE EYRE UNCOVERED

by

CHRISTOPHER PETER GREY

THE INNOVATIVE GUIDE FOR
A-LEVEL STUDENTS

***

PLOT SUMMARY, ANALYSIS,
IDEAS, AND COMMENTARY

SECTION I

JANE EYRE STORYLINE - MAIN EVENTS

CHAPTERS 1 - 4

JANE AT GATESHEAD HALL (years 0-10)

- "My father had been a poor clergyman...my mother had married him against the wishes of her friends..."
- Jane's mother and father both die of typhus fever
- Jane is brought up by the Reeds at Gateshead Hall (Mr Reed was the brother of Jane's mother; he dies soon after his sister)
- Mrs Reed resents Jane's presence
- Jane fights with John Reed, the son, and is spurned by the sisters, Georgiana and Eliza
- Jane is forced to enter the red-room as punishment
- Visit by Mr Brocklehurst of Lowood School to assess Jane
- Jane's tirade against her aunt, Mrs Reed
- Jane sent to Lowood

CHAPTERS 5 - 10

JANE AT LOWOOD SCHOOL (years 10-18)

- Two key figures: the teacher, Miss Temple, the first person to show Jane kindness; the pupil, Helen Burns, whose Christian principle of submission is set against Jane's survival instincts and struggle for personal justice
- Helen Burns dies of typhus; Miss Temple leaves to get married
- Jane leaves Lowood

CHAPTERS 11 - 20

JANE AT THORNFIELD HALL (years 18-19)

- Mrs Fairfax, the housekeeper
- Jane hears peculiar laughter (Bertha); sees Grace Poole, Bertha's minder

- Jane's first encounter with Rochester (after his horse falls)
- Jane and Rochester's growing closeness
- Bertha sets fire to Rochester's room; Jane saves him
- Rochester leaves Thornfield to visit friends (10 days)
- Rochester and company return to Thornfield (Blanche Ingram + Rochester)
- Jane recognises that Rochester does not love Blanche
- Richard Mason (Bertha's brother) arrives at Thornfield
- Rochester disguises himself as a gypsy woman to tell fortunes
- Mason badly wounded by Bertha; Rochester employs Jane to nurse him
- Mason sent away secretly to avoid explanations

CHAPTERS 21 – 22

JANE RETURNS TO GATESHEAD

- Jane summoned to Gateshead Hall by request of Mrs Reed, who is terminally ill
- Jane meets Eliza and Georgiana again (John is dead, suspected suicide)
- Jane meets Mrs Reed again; she is unwilling to soften towards Jane
- After ten days, Mrs Reed admits that she received a letter (three years before) from Jane's uncle, John Eyre, who wanted to bequeath his fortune to her; Mrs Reed never told Jane and wrote to Eyre to tell him she was dead
- Jane forgives Mrs Reed; she does not return the blessing
- Mrs Reed dies unmourned by her daughters
- Jane leaves Gateshead after a month, yearning to see Rochester

CHAPTERS 22 – 27

JANE RETURNS TO THORNFIELD

- Rochester continues to allow Jane to believe he will marry Blanche. A fortnight passes.
- It is midsummer when Rochester at last reveals to Jane that he loves her, after she makes an impassioned speech to him in the orchard, declaring that they are "equals"

- Rochester's admission of love causes agreeable changes in Jane
- Rochester wants to marry within four weeks
- Preparations are made for the wedding; Jane is very much in love, but she resists being treated like a bride-to-be and has difficulty believing it is not all a dream
- Mrs Fairfax is notified (she is sceptical that it will work out)
- For the first time in Jane's life, her love for a man - Rochester - eclipses her love for God
- Bertha invades Jane's room at night and rips her bridal veil in two; Jane passes out in terror; the next day, Rochester, continuing to conceal Bertha's existence, insists it was only a bad dream
- The wedding day is interrupted by the arrival of the solicitor, Briggs, and Richard Mason, who proclaim that Rochester already has a wife
- Rochester at last admits to the existence of Bertha in Jane's presence
- Rochester reveals Bertha's room
- Jane is cleared of blame; the impending marriage became known to Richard Mason through his business dealings with Jane's uncle, John Eyre, to whom Jane has now written after the revelations of Mrs Reed; Mr Eyre is very ill
- Jane is devastated by Rochester's duplicity; she blames her own weakness; she turns back to God for succour
- Jane resolves that she must leave Thornfield directly; Rochester tries to dissuade her, alternating threats with pleading and self-pity; Jane is resolute
- Rochester tells Jane the story of his marriage to Bertha: how she went "mad"; how he brought her back to England and locked her up; how he travelled around Europe and had affairs with other women
- Rochester tells Jane that meeting her has changed his life and that he does not want to part with her; Jane will not surrender to him; he, in a fury, tries to restrain her physically from leaving - but only briefly, realising that it would be a terrible error to hurt her
- Jane spends one more night at Thornfield and leaves very early the next day, distressed and remorseful, without telling Rochester

CHAPTERS 28 - 35

JANE AND THE RIVERS FAMILY (years 19-20)

- Jane is dropped off from her coach at Whitcross, alone and without resources. She spends the night outdoors on the moor. The next day she looks for help at a village, but is mostly turned away. She again enters the wilderness of the moors.
- Exhausted and desperate, she comes across Moor House, where the Rivers family lives. St John Rivers permits her to enter. There are two sisters, Diana and Mary. Jane calls herself "Jane Elliott" to hide her identity.
- Jane grows close to Diana and Mary, but not so with St John, who is the parish priest; though he is distant and severe, Jane respects him.
- St John offers her a post as teacher at the village school. News arrives of the death of the Rivers' uncle, John.
- Jane struggles to find satisfaction at the school, but determines to do her best.
- Jane suffers when she thinks of Rochester and the life she might have had with him. He is a recurrent subject of her dreams.
- St John tells Jane that he has now found his path in life and plans to become a missionary. He is in love with Rosamond Oliver, the daughter of the local business magnate, but will not permit himself to reveal his feelings.
- Jane meets Rosamond's father, who compliments her on her work at the school. He thinks that if St John becomes a missionary he will waste his life.
- Jane has drawn a study of Rosamond, which St John sees. He confesses he loves Rosamond, but considers her unsuitable. As St John leaves, he tears off a corner of the drawing, on which Jane has signed her name.
- The next day, St John returns and shows Jane her signature: she has signed herself "Jane Eyre" instead of "Jane Elliott". St John announces that she is the inheritor of her recently deceased uncle John Eyre of Madeira's fortune, concerning which St John has been notified by Mr Briggs, the solicitor. Jane has inherited £20,000. St John tells Jane that Rochester has disappeared.

- St John also reveals that they are cousins; Jane is ecstatic to discover that she has a family and tells St John she wishes to divide the inheritance equally among them. St John tries to dissuade her, but she is adamant. Eventually everything is settled, and it is arranged that the inheritance will be split between the four cousins.
- Jane busies herself preparing Moor House for Christmas and the return of Diana and Mary from their posts as governesses. St John announces that he will leave England within the next year. Separately, Rosamond Oliver has announced her engagement; St John shows no reaction.
- St John persuades Jane to study Hindustani (preparing her to accompany him to India); he pushes her relentlessly in her studies.
- One day, he takes Jane for a walk and proposes that she travel with him – as his wife. Jane resists; St John argues his case. At last she agrees to go – but as his aide only. St John rejects this idea. He tries to coerce her into submitting, but Jane is equal to him and will not surrender to his pressure. The same evening, he once more assails her, going so far as to imply that God will condemn her if she does not obey him.
- Jane, on the verge of giving in to St John, hears Rochester's voice calling her; she breaks free from St John's spell, dismisses him, and intends to go immediately to Rochester. Jane has been with the Rivers family for a year.

CHAPTER 36 – 38

RETURN TO THORNFIELD – REUNION WITH ROCHESTER

- St John tries a final time to influence Jane, but this fails. Jane travels directly to Thornfield, which she finds ruined and abandoned. At the inn, she is told by the keeper about the fire, how it was started by Bertha, and how Rochester was badly injured, losing his sight and the use of a hand. Jane arranges to be taken to him immediately.
- Jane arrives at Ferndean, his house, where Rochester is cared for by his former servants, John and Mary. When Jane identifies herself to Rochester, he undergoes a sequence of highly emotional reactions.

- They are soon married (and at the time of telling her story, they have been married for ten years and have a child, a boy). The sight in one of Rochester's eyes gradually returns. Diana and Mary both find husbands. St John remains in India, unmarried. The story ends with a letter from St John alluding to an eventual meeting with God after death - and welcoming that day.

SECTION II

*DETAILED PLOT AND MAIN CHARACTER ANALYSIS
WITH ADDITIONAL COMMENTS, NOTES, IDEAS, & THEORIES*

VOL. I

STAGE ONE: CHILDHOOD WITH MRS REED & FAMILY

Chapter 1

"There was no possibility of taking a walk that day."

Such an interesting opening line. So matter-of-fact, so nondescript. There is a dividing line in Jane's life between the mundane facts of her existence, the rules and regulations that confine her throughout her childhood and adolescence (firstly with Mrs Reed, then at Lowood), and her highly creative and visionary imagination, which manifests itself in her drawings, her dreams, and her yearning for connection with something bigger than herself, something universal (her first connection is with God, then with love for Rochester).

Jane is reading Bewick's *History of British Birds.* This is not insignificant. Birds have freedom, independence, the ability to choose where they make their home: all things Jane yearns for and cannot achieve until she is much older.

Mrs Reed's son, John, protected by his mother's blind devotion to him (it is Mrs Reed's undoing in the end) bullies and derides Jane: "You are a dependant, mama says; you have no money; your father left you none; you ought to beg, and not to live here with gentlemen's children like us, and eat the same meals we do, and wear clothes at our mama's expense." (Oppressed from childhood, forced to obey people who disrespect and undervalue her, Jane must conserve and hold onto her inner strength for many years before she can realise her true self: she is in every way the definition of a heroine, someone who overcomes multiple obstacles before achieving freedom and fulfillment.)

In spite of John's harassment, Jane does not take his unkindness mutely – her pride will not allow it. In an early example of her unyielding character, she cries out: "Wicked and cruel boy!...You are like a murderer – you are like a slave-driver – you are like the Roman emperors!" John Reed launches himself at her, and Jane fights back; this fierce retaliation results in Jane being consigned to the red-room.

Chapter 2

THE RED-ROOM

"I resisted all the way: a new thing for me...I was a trifle beside myself; or rather *out* of myself, as the French would say..." Jane gives the reader a first example of her future refusals to back down under attack, which she will demonstrate throughout the story when confronted with attempts by males to dominate her (Brocklehurst, Rochester, St John Rivers).

Bessie, one of the servants at Gateshead Hall, the Reeds' house, scolds Jane after this incident: "...it is your place to be humble...", she says. This is advice that Jane will shun, because she does not recognise her "place" amongst the Reed family. Indeed, Jane *has* no place; until she finds Rochester, she is an outsider, with no home, no family (even her attempt to make the Rivers siblings her "family" does not entirely succeed). Rochester becomes her home, her sanctuary, her destiny.

Jane's imagination is always active, we discover: her sparkling intelligence manifests itself both positively in her creative side (drawing, describing, dreaming) and also, when it is subverted by adverse circumstances, turned against herself with a harsh negative force in the form of very personal attacks on her looks and status. In this chapter, when she is restrained by the servants after fighting back against John Reed, Jane gives us a striking instance of the imaginative damage she can do to herself, when she entertains the thought of "never eating or drinking more, and letting myself die."

This thought is swiftly followed by the first of many negative attacks directed against herself: "…had I been a sanguine, brilliant, careless, exacting, handsome, romping child…" Jane has a recurring tendency to put herself down, which runs throughout her life until she and Rochester are finally settled and she finds mental equilibrium (positive and negative in balance). Note, as you read the story, how many times Jane bluntly refers to how *unattractive* she is. Whenever she is in a state of emotional turmoil, her thoughts become poisonous. There are many examples of this self-flagellation throughout the book, and they tend to occur when Jane feels vulnerable and unwanted. Perhaps - we can only propose it as a theory - Bronte herself was like this. When Jane meets Rochester, this kind of thought disappears; and when she loses him, after the failed marriage, the thoughts start up again.

Jane is locked into the red-room. Bronte hyphenates the two words, which is unusual; she might have called it the Red Room, drawing attention to its significance by using capitals, but instead she has found a more interesting way of highlighting the location's importance in the story through joining, as with a cable or rope - methods of restraint - the words "red" and "room", ingeniously demonstrating how two common, separately insignificant words, when locked together with a hyphen, take on a very powerful, even forbidding, aura of enclosure and threat.

Inside this locked room, which is where Mrs Reed's husband lay ill and eventually died, Jane's youthful imagination runs riot: "…a light gleamed on the wall…I thought the swift-darting beam was a herald of some coming vision from another world." *The red-room sequence has many possible thematic interpretations (and many critics have shared their own), but let us point out one possibly useful, original idea: when this situation becomes too overwhelming for Jane, she cries out to be released from the room and is refused - and then she loses consciousness. There is one other time when this happens, this loss of consciousness: when Bertha finds her way into Jane's room and tears up her bridal veil the night before the wedding to Rochester. What connects these two events? The fear of losing her mind, Jane's most precious asset; rather than continue to allow the mental assault to be prolonged, she simply shuts off to preserve her mental integrity.*

Chapter 3

Jane reads *Gulliver's Travels*, which (like Bewick's *Birds*) has some significance. Gulliver - like Jane - twice finds himself in societies where he is out of place: in Lilliput he is a giant while the populace is tiny; in Brobdignag he is tiny while the populace is gigantic. Jane, too, finds it difficult to be the right size (i.e., comfortable with others) until she finds Rochester.

"Children can feel, but they cannot analyze their feelings..." An astute observation. Children can only display raw emotion; they are as yet unable to regulate or make sense of their emotions. Jane tells her story when she is approximately thirty years old and can look back on her behaviour as a child and reflect on it with maturity.

When Jane is at last released from the red-room, she overhears Abbot the servant as much as saying that she deserved no pity for being confined such a long time, simply because she is not very attractive. As Abbot says: "if she were a nice, pretty child...", implying that cuteness would have meant an earlier release, topping it off with: "one cannot really care for such a little toad..."

Bronte's opening scenes clearly demonstrate to the reader how hostile Jane's childhood environment is; "children can feel", yes, and what they hear, what is told to them – especially what is hurtful, is stored up and remembered for all time.

Chapter 4

Jane reflects on why she fought back against John Reed and was made to suffer for it. She recognises the unjustness of her treatment, and it foments "deep ire and desperate revolt" inside her. She thinks to herself: "…it seemed as if my tongue pronounced words without my will consenting to their utterance: something spoke out of me over which I had no control." This uncontrollable rebelliousness comes from Jane's powerful mental energy, which explodes when she feels she is being treated unfairly (there are similar instances with Rochester and St John Rivers).

Mrs Reed summons Mr Brocklehurst, the principal of Lowood School, whence she intends to send Jane so that she does not have to deal with her any longer.

During the interview, Jane, while outwardly humble, shows flashes of the ironic wit which pops up from time to time in her conversation. This exchange is an amusing – as well as daring – response for a child of only ten years, especially when confronted with a figure as forbidding as Brocklehurst, who towers over Jane in a black frock coat like "a black pillar" .

Brocklehurst: "What is hell?"
Jane: "A pit full of fire."
Brocklehurst: "What must you do to avoid it?"
Jane: "Keep in good health, and not die."

After Brocklehurst leaves (having handed out to Jane some cautionary pamphlet about the dangers of lying), Jane, still smarting from the injustice she feels she has been dealt, goes on the attack again, this time against Mrs Reed. Jane knows she is going to be sent away to Lowood, so for her there is no reason to withhold her scorn any longer.

"Speak I must," Jane thinks to herself; "I had been trodden on severely, and *must* turn…" Jane then lashes out with all her verbal fury:

"I am not deceitful: if I were, I should say I loved *you*; but I declare I do not love you: I dislike you the worst of anybody in the world except John Reed; and this book about the liar, you may give to your girl, Georgiana, for it is she who tells lies, and not I."

Following this initial outburst, Jane feels exhilarated; she is "thrilled with ungovernable excitement", which encourages her to continue with the assault on Mrs Reed:

"I am glad you are no relation of mine: I will never call you aunt again as long as I live. I will never come to see you when I am grown up; and if any one asks me how I liked you, and how you treated me, I will say the very thought of you makes me sick, and that you treated me with miserable cruelty."

And then Jane adds:

"You think I have no feelings, and that I can do without one bit of love or kindness; but I cannot live so: and you have no pity."

Concluding with:

"People think you are a good woman, but you are bad; hard-hearted. *You* are deceitful!"

Releasing more of this negative energy that has been suppressed for so long inside her, Jane delights in the relief of delivering the truth to her guardian:

"...my soul began to expand, to exult, with the strangest sense of freedom, of triumph, I ever felt."

This is an important moment in Jane's life. It marks the point at which she finds the courage to fight back against the forces of oppression that have been ranged against her since she was born. Having done this once, she will be able to do it again in the future when she feels unfairly treated.

"I was left there alone - winner of the field. It was the hardest battle I had fought, and the first victory I have gained..."

Chapter 5

STAGE TWO: LOWOOD

Jane is despatched to Lowood, which is as "low" as its name: icily cold, drearily inhospitable, and so miserly with the food rations that the pupils are constantly hungry (especially the younger ones, whose portions get snatched by "the great girls"); Brocklehurst justifies this in the name of "mortifying the flesh" of young women. Like all tyrants, he is eventually exposed as a hypocrite: while he enjoys denying his pupils, he and his family live very well off the school.

However, despite all the school's deprivations, there is a teacher, Miss Temple, who begins to take an interest in Jane, who in turn comes to revere her. And although, at the beginning of her years at Lowood, Jane is entirely alone, she reminds herself "to that feeling of isolation I was accustomed..." It is no worse than being at Gateshead with the Reeds. Jane must combat this feeling of isolation all her life until she finds Rochester.

Chapter 6

Jane admires her fellow pupil, Helen Burns, who later dies of consumption at the school (just as Charlotte Bronte's two older sisters, Maria and Elizabeth, died from similar conditions caught at their own boarding school). Helen is the image of the Christian martyr who never complains, never fights back (unlike Jane), and suffers everything doled out to her because she is prepared - indeed, eager for - death, in order to be reunited with God. She is the opposite of Jane, who will *not* take oppression and unjust treatment as if they were her destiny.

Bronte draws a stark contrast between the Evangelicalism of Helen Burns and the more conventional Christian faith of Jane Eyre (the Evangelical movement was popular in mid-19th c. England).

Helen chastises Jane for wanting to fight back, saying that it is Jane's duty "to bear it, if you could not avoid it: it is weak and silly to say you *cannot bear* what it is your fate to be required to bear." Jane does not condone such an attitude, even though she admires it, believing that Helen "considered things by a light invisible to my eyes." Jane, in that severe and self-effacing way she has, regards her own nature, when compared with Helen's, as "wretchedly defective."

Helen does not make any effort to change what are perceived by the school staff as her faults. Jane tries to help her, saying "it is so easy to be careful", but Helen is not interested; she has no desire to amend her behaviour when her creed is one of suffering every blow gratefully. Jane has learned how to avoid punishment, however, and only resists authority when she believes that she is the victim of *injustice*. For example, speaking of the bullying Miss Scatcherd, she thinks: "if she struck me with that rod, I should get it from her hand; I should break it under her nose." This is where Jane differs from Helen – and where Charlotte Bronte wants to make the point that strict religious interpretation (if someone hits you on one side, tell her to hit the other) is *not for her*. Bronte's father, it is universally known, was a parish priest and a very pious man. In *Jane Eyre*, Charlotte Bronte questions, if not repudiates, what may well have been the doctrine of her own father. Even if that is not entirely the case, this argument between Helen and Jane – between Helen's meek compliance and Jane's fiery resistance – continues for many lines, indicating the importance of the discussion to Bronte. As Jane powerfully affirms:

"When we are struck at without a reason, we should strike back again very hard; I am sure we should – so hard as to teach the person who struck us never to do it again." And: "I must dislike those who, whatever I do to please them, persist in disliking me; I must resist those who punish me unjustly."

However, Helen rebuts this philosophy. For her, "heathens and savage tribes hold that doctrine; but Christians and civilized nations disown it. ...It is not violence that best overcomes hate – nor vengeance that most certainly heals injury. ...read the New Testament and observe what Christ says, and how he acts – make his word your rule, and his conduct your example. ...Love your enemies; bless them that curse you; do good to them that hate you... Life appears to me too short to be spent in nursing animosity, or registering wrongs. We are, and must be, one and all, burdened with faults in this world: but the time will soon come when, I trust, we shall put them off in putting off our corruptible bodies; when debasement and sin will fall from us with this cumbrous frame of flesh, and only the spark of the spirit will remain, – the impalpable principle of life and thought, pure as when it left the Creator to inspire the creature: whence it came it will return; perhaps again to be communicated to some being higher than man ... it makes Eternity a rest - a mighty home, not a terror and an abyss. ...I live in calm, looking to the end."

It is a long speech - certainly as long as any delivered by Jane during the course of the book - so the reader may infer that the contents are of some importance to the author, which is why the full length is here set down. The question is, therefore, whether Charlotte Bronte agrees with Helen's pious stance, or whether Jane's viewpoint (return a blow twice as hard as you receive it) is the author's preferred philosophy. There is no certain answer, of course, but we may note that Helen dies prematurely, her potential unfulfilled - and Jane goes on to live a fruitful, and, in the end, happy life. The only way Jane eventually succeeds in achieving the life she wants is to show determination, courage, and resistance - not to back down, give up, and take life's blows without fighting back. So maybe Bronte *was* telling us which side she was on.

Chapter 7

Mr Brocklehurst, the principal, pays a visit to Lowood School. Jane reserves a particular venom for Brocklehurst, who is the dark side of piety, an anti-Helen Burns. Whereas Helen is good, kind, uncorrupted, Brocklehurst is a sadist, a hypocrite, and a bully - yet both consider themselves devout Christians.

When Miss Temple complains that the children were that morning given an inedible breakfast, Brocklehurst spits back:

"Oh, madam, when you put bread and cheese, instead of burnt porridge into these children's mouths, you may indeed feed their vile bodies, but you little think how you starve their immortal souls!"

And when Miss Temple tries to reason with him, he continues: "Madam, I have a Master to serve whose kingdom is not of this world: my mission is to mortify in these girls the lusts of the flesh..."

Soon after this, Brocklehurst's wife and daughters enter the hall, and they are decked out in expensive clothes and fashionable coiffure. Bronte's amusingly satirical portrait of the hypocritical Brocklehurst scarcely masks her deep antipathy for such people who claim to be good Christians and act more like tyrants. Clearly she knew the type well.

Brocklehurst is particularly hateful towards Jane, because he recognises someone who sees through his facade of devotional piety and right into his blackened heart. To the assembled school, he points to Jane and asks: "Who would think that the Evil One had already found a servant and agent in her? Yet such, I grieve to say, is the case." He then calls her "…a little castaway…an interloper and an alien", tells the whole school to "avoid her company", and tops off his attack with "this girl is - a liar!"

Having loudly humiliated Jane before the assembly, Brocklehurst makes her stand on a stool for everyone to stare at. When the assembly disperses, Helen Burns comes to the rescue, to Jane's immense gratitude:

"It was as if a martyr, a hero, had passed a slave or victim, and imparted strength in the transit. I mastered the rising hysteria, lifted up my head, and took a firm stand on the stool. ….[Helen] smiled at me as she again went by. What a smile! I remember it now, and I know that it was the effluence of fine intellect, of true courage…like a reflection from the aspect of an angel."

Bronte gives us two contrary versions of Christianity to consider: Helen the gentle pacifist and Brocklehurst the belligerent bully. We know also that Jane, our heroine, charts a middle course in her life, believing in God, praising Him and thanking Him, but not using Him either as a weapon to wound herself, like Helen - or hurt others, like Brocklehurst.

Chapter 8

After Brocklehurst's public shaming, Jane suffers a mental setback:

"I had meant to be so good, and to do so much at Lowood; to make so many friends, to earn respect, and win affection…that very morning I had reached the head of my class; Miss Miller had praised me warmly; Miss Temple had smiled approbation…I was well received by my fellow-pupils; treated as an equal by those of my own age, and not molested by any: now, here I lay crushed and trodden on; and could I ever rise more?"

Helen comes to comfort and reassure her: "If all the world hated you, and believed you wicked, while your own conscience approved you, and absolved you from guilt, you would not be without friends" (i.e., your conscience is your friend – if you have done the right thing).

Jane responds: "…if others don't love me, I would rather die than live…I cannot bear to be solitary and hated, Helen."

And, once more, Helen is given a lengthy speech in which she expounds the "good Christian" philosophy:

"Hush, Jane! You think too much of the love of human beings; you are too impulsive, too vehement: the sovereign hand that created your frame, and put life into it, has provided you with other resources than your feeble self, or than creatures feeble as you. …there is an invisible world and a kingdom of spirits: that world is round us, for it is everywhere; and those spirits watch us, for they are commissioned to guard us; and if we were dying in pain and shame, if scorn smote us on all sides, and hatred crushed us, angels see our tortures, recognise our innocence…and God waits only for the separation of spirit from flesh to crown us with a full reward. Why, then, should we ever sink overwhelmed with distress, when life is so soon over, and death is so certain an entrance to happiness – to glory?"

Again, the idea that life is nothing more than a brief, unhappy prelude to everlasting joy after death (and therefore should not be treated with such seriousness as Jane imparts to it) is given a full exposition by Helen, and this time it is filled with the fanciful imagery of ministering "spirits" and "angels", adding a poetic embellishment to the stark message. Even Evangelicalism needs a sweetener to hold the faithful in its grasp.

Helen uses the word "feeble" twice when describing mankind; much later in the story, St John Rivers, another evangelical, uses the word in the phrase "feeble fellow-worms". *Feeble* is exactly what Jane is *not*: her motivations and actions refute the idea propounded by the pious of the era that human beings have no agency, no personal power, and no *right* to act in any way that benefits them as individuals.

As noted before, Bronte's father was a priest, and a devout one, and the Bronte children were no doubt subjected to the Christian doctrine, and perhaps an extreme version of it, like Helen's. We can observe Bronte using Helen, Brocklehurst, and, later, St John Rivers in opposition to Jane's credo in order to present the various aspects of Christianity in a kind of roundtable discussion, the kind that must have been revolving inside Bronte's head and seeking a resolution. Throughout *Jane Eyre*, Bronte appears to be arguing with herself about the merits of Christianity through her characters. The crucial point is that Jane wants to be happy *while she lives* – that is why she never gives up on Rochester. Charlotte Bronte, too, wanted to get married, which she eventually did after much ambivalence and procrastination, but, sadly, not for long: she died the year after her marriage.

Now it is Helen Burns's turn to be humiliated by the school: she is obliged to stand with a sign around her neck, on which is written "Slattern" (untidy, lazy person). Jane, however, does not adhere to Helen's previous advice to meekly suffer any indignity, removes the sign – and throws it in the fire, thinking to herself as she does this that "the fury of which she [Helen] was incapable had been burning in my soul all day, and tears, hot and large, had continually been scalding my cheek; for the spectacle of her sad resignation gave me an intolerable pain at the heart". Helen surrenders – Jane fights back.

Later on, the accusations which Brocklehurst brought against Jane as a result of what Mrs Reed had told him are dismissed after an investigation by Miss Temple, who announces her conclusion to the school that Jane is "completely cleared from every imputation" of wrongdoing. Jane has been vindicated, and she is very relieved, thinking that "I would not now have exchanged Lowood with all its privations, for Gateshead and its daily luxuries…".

Chapter 9

Spring comes to Lowood, bringing typhus. 45 of the 80 girls become ill. Many die. Bronte draws the contrast between the fine weather outside and the fatal disease within. Brocklehurst, instead of going to the school and offering every assistance as the responsible authority, shuns it.

As if it was pre-destined that Helen Burns should die young and be reunited with her God, she becomes very ill from consumption (tuberculosis). Jane ruminates: "Helen Burns was numbering her last days in this world...she was going to be taken to the region of spirits, if such region there were." We should pay particular attention to that last phrase: *if such region there were.* What are we to make of that? It is a short phrase, almost an afterthought, and yet, to this reader, it has the weight of a cathedral bell and is just as loud. It signals the doubt that is growing in Jane's mind concerning a fundamental Christian belief – the hereafter, the afterlife. Jane sees her friend dying, witnesses the injustice of it, and she begins to have second thoughts about Christian doctrine. For if Helen, a good and gifted person, can die so young, so prematurely, so *unfairly* – well, if God can allow that to happen, then perhaps He does not have such control over the world as his devotees claim. And if *that* is the case, then maybe Paradise and Eternity alike are a fantasy, a sham, a story invented to keep people mute and malleable and compliant. As Jane tells us:

"And then my mind made its first earnest effort to comprehend what had been infused into it concerning heaven and hell: and for the first time it recoiled, baffled; and for the first time glancing behind, on each side, and before it, it saw all round an unfathomed gulf: it felt the one point where it stood – the present; all the rest was formless cloud and vacant depth: and it shuddered at the thought of tottering, and plunging amid that chaos."

Unlike Helen, who has no doubts about the reception she will get afterwards, Jane is not looking forward to death: she cannot visualize the paradise that Helen imagines is waiting for her. Sitting at Helen's bedside, Jane asks her: "Are you going somewhere, Helen? Are you going home?" Helen responds: "Yes; to my long home – my last home." She continues: "I am very happy, Jane; and when you hear that I am dead you must be sure and not grieve: there is nothing to grieve about. ...I leave no one to regret me much: I have only a father; and he is lately married, and will not miss me. By dying young I shall escape great sufferings. I had not qualities or talents to make my way very well in the world: I should have been continually at fault."

Is it the promise of a happy eternity that Helen longs for, or just the exit from an *unhappy* life? The key lies in the phrase "I have only a father…and [he] will not miss me." Helen's father will not miss her if she *dies*? What kind of father – or *man* - is he? And what kind of parent has he been to Helen that the only comfort or affection in her life has come from an indeterminate figure called God? No wonder she has abandoned any hope of happiness on earth and looks to the afterlife in the hope of discovering it there!

Helen and Jane have a final exchange. Note that Helen refers to God here as a "mighty, universal Parent" – the loving parent that her own father has failed to be.

Helen: I believe; I have faith; I am going to God.
Jane: Where is God? What is God?
Helen: My Maker and yours; who will never destroy what he has created. I am sure there is a future state; I believe God is good; I can resign my immortal part to him without any misgiving. God is my father; God is my friend; I love him; I believe he loves me.
Jane: And shall I see you again, Helen, when I die?
Helen: You will come to the same region of happiness: be received by the same mighty, universal Parent…

Helen dies during the night.

But is Jane convinced by Helen's certainty of her posthumous departure for a "region of happiness", or has her death only made Jane more certain that she has to make her own life mean something, because there is *nothing* afterwards? It is an argument that continues throughout *Jane Eyre*, and it is ambiguously resolved at the end of the story. Jane concludes Helen's sad life:

"Her grave is in Brocklehurst churchyard: for fifteen years after her death it was only covered by a grassy mound; but now a gray marble tablet marks the spot, inscribed with her name, and the word "Resurgam"'.

Resurgam: I shall rise again. One wonders if Jane paid for the headstone with her inheritance. There is no question, on reflection. It could only have been Jane.

Chapter 10

Eight years pass by at Lowood School; Jane ceases being a pupil at 16 and has now been teaching there for two years.

After the typhus outbreak has done its work at Lowood and finally dispersed, there is an "inquiry" amidst "public indignation" at the death of so many girls. Improvements are made at last, and Brocklehurst is removed from the school administration. Amongst the pleasing changes at the school, Jane experiences "a desire to excel". Meanwhile, there is no communication from Mrs Reed or her family.

Miss Temple marries and leaves. Jane records that it is to "an excellent man, almost worthy of such a wife…" But nothing is the same afterwards. Jane reappraises her situation and, like most young people would do, finds that she longs for more contact with the outside world:

"…I had undergone a transforming process…beginning to feel the stirring of old emotions…it was not the power to be tranquil which had failed me, but the reason for tranquillity was no more…now I remembered that the real world was wide, and that a varied field of hopes and fears, of sensation and excitement, awaited those who had courage to go forth into its expanse to seek real knowledge of life amidst its perils."

She sums it up by thinking: "…those most remote, those blue peaks: it was those I longed to surmount…" Who has not felt like that at age 18?

Always seeking, never settling, never surrendering: these are the principles which guide and propel Jane forward to meet her destiny. "I tired of the routine of eight years in one afternoon. I desired liberty; for liberty I gasped; for liberty I uttered a prayer…"

In the autumn, Jane decides to advertise. A reply comes from a Mrs Fairfax of Thornfield Hall near Millcote. Jane is awarded the post of governess.

Before Jane departs, there is a visit from a Gateshead servant, Bessie. The purpose of this is really plot-driven, to tell Jane of an incident "nearly seven years ago", when "a Mr Eyre came to Gateshead...he was your father's brother." Jane was at Lowood when he arrived, and Mrs Reed kept the information about Jane's location under her bonnet.

Once again - and again it happens during a period of transition for Jane, when she is at her most vulnerable - the reader is exposed to Jane's inherent self-criticism. Bessie inspects Jane, and her glance "did in no shape denote admiration." Then Bessie says, without provocation, "you were no beauty as a child". Jane, of course, is wounded: "...at eighteen most people wish to please, and the conviction that they have not an exterior likely to second that desire brings anything but gratification." A mannered way of saying that such criticism is very hurtful, which of course it is, especially at that age. But whereas Jane would have responded in kind to any other kind of attack - she would undoubtedly have retaliated! - a personal comment on her looks causes her to shrink back. Her appearance is not something she feels she can defend.

This sensitivity about her looks undermines Jane throughout her life until she settles down with Rochester - there are so many moments in the story when the reader is caught short by yet another instance of Jane underlining her own unattractiveness (as she sees it). Rochester, however, finds her appealing enough, because he falls in love first with her mind and her attitude - and then her face begins to draw him in, too. With Rochester, Jane can argue about looks (he is the only one with whom she can, because she feels comfortable with him), and on at least two occasions says - to his face - that he is not at all handsome.

Jane Eyre is a very modern heroine in respect of her self-criticism: there is scarcely a literary heroine today who doesn't draw attention to her own failings, either in terms of looks, habits, or prospects (Bridget Jones, perhaps the most popular of all contemporary heroines, being a prime example). But

Jane was there first, directly addressing the reader while exposing her insecurities and sharing her anxieties, demanding attention and empathy. What is more, by the end of the story Bronte has found an ingenious way to ensure that Jane's biggest fears are laid to rest (more on that later). We might well call Jane "Literature's First Feminist" - she doesn't let how she (thinks she) looks or her harsh childhood interfere with her aim to take on the world, enlarge her existence, create, and be an individual - she fights back against her given circumstances and does not relent until she has gained what she wants. That was something extraordinary in 1847.

Chapter 11

STAGE THREE: THORNFIELD AND ROCHESTER

Jane arrives at Thornfield, meets Mrs Fairfax the housekeeper and Adele Varens, who will be her pupil. Straightaway, we see that Thornfield is a creepy kind of structure much favoured in the Gothic literature movement of late 18th-early 19th Century. Jane mentions "the eerie impression made by that wide hall, that dark and spacious staircase, and that long, cold gallery..."

But these uncanny feelings (vibrations from Bertha's presence upstairs, no doubt) do not diminish Jane's optimism, which consists mainly in having made her escape from Lowood:

"Externals have a great effect on the young: I thought that a fairer era of life was beginning for me, one that was to have its flowers and pleasures, as well as its thorns and toils. My faculties, roused by the change of scene, the new field offered to hope, seemed all astir. I cannot precisely define what they expected, but it was something pleasant: not perhaps that day or that month, but at an indefinite future period."

This is the glory of being young - the feeling of anticipation, even for something undefinable - the sense that the world is about to reveal itself to you. However, in this new and unfamiliar setting (where Jane at first feels out of her depth and vulnerable), the old (and oddly comforting) feelings of inferiority return to offset the hope of the future:

"...I ever wished to look as well as I could, and to please as much as my want of beauty would permit. I sometimes regretted that I was not handsomer: I sometimes wished to have rosy cheeks, a straight nose, and small cherry mouth; I desired to be tall, stately and finely developed in figure; I felt it a misfortune that I was so little, so pale, and had features so irregular and so marked. And why had I these aspirations and these regrets? It would be difficult to say: I could not then distinctly say it to myself; yet I had a reason, and a logical, natural reason too."

(The "logical, natural reason" she alludes to is that she wants to be desired sexually, but she does not have the nerve – rather, it was not permissible to write such a brazen thing in a book published in 1847 – to say it out loud. But we know what she is thinking. It is a brave confession, even in such oblique language, to admit that you want to be wanted, and that being attractive gets you attention.)

Jane instantly feels at home with Mrs Fairfax, once she is made aware that the latter is not the owner of Thornfield, but a simple employee: "this affable and kind little widow was no great dame, but a dependant like myself...The equality between her and me was real...my position was all the freer."

Equality is a very important word for Jane: she has been seeking it all her life. What is equality but a state of fair play, which Jane has never had until her arrival at Thornfield? Indeed, as in the section quoted above, she comes to Thornfield thinking "a fairer era of life" is beginning for her.

Jane asks about Mr Rochester (she has not met him yet), and Mrs Fairfax describes him:

"...he has a gentleman's taste and habits. And he expects to have things managed in conformity to them."
"...his character is unimpeachable, I suppose. He is rather peculiar, perhaps...I dare say he is clever...you cannot be always sure whether he is in jest or earnest, whether he is pleased or the contrary...
"...he is a very good master."

"Unimpeachable, I suppose", states Mrs Fairfax. Her addition of "I suppose" hints at the damning revelations that will be duly disclosed to the reader about the master of Thornfield. Far from being unimpeachable, Rochester will reveal himself as a sinner of the first rank.

THE FIRST SIGN OF BERTHA'S PRESENCE AT THORNFIELD: Jane hears "a laugh...distinct, formal, mirthless" as Mrs Fairfax is showing her round the house; she tells Jane it is "perhaps Grace Poole" (one of the servants). Jane hears it again: "The laugh was repeated in its low, syllabic tone, and terminated in an odd murmur...as tragic, as preternatural a laugh as any I ever heard..." And then Grace Poole emerges from the room they are passing at that moment – but this is pure misdirection on the part of the author: Bronte wants us to think it is Grace Poole with the goblin laugh, until she is ready to reveal Bertha.

Chapter 12

Jane settles in to Thornfield House and is tolerably content. But there is a dissatisfaction inside her, a yearning for more:

"Anybody may blame me who like, when I add further, that, now and then…
I climbed the three staircases, raised the trap-door of the attic, and having reached the leads, looked out afar over sequestered field and hill, and along dim sky-line: that then I longed for a power of vision which might overpass that limit; which might reach the busy world, towns, regions full of life I had heard of but never seen: that then I desired more of practical experience than I possessed; more of intercourse with my kind, of acquaintance with variety of character, than was here within my reach. …I believed in the existence of other and more vivid kinds of goodness, and what I believed in I wished to behold."

*Here Jane speaks for herself and also for the thousands of women who would read **Jane Eyre** over the next two centuries and have those same feelings of being confined to a life that was inadequate to their desires: of being undervalued and overlooked. Women in the era of **Jane Eyre** were customarily not meant to possess "a power of vision"; they were meant to* *concern themselves with domesticity and household tasks, and Jane knows that by voicing the desire for a life of wider scope and possibility, she might well be encouraging censure from the patriarchy (government, church, the wealthy), whose job it was to ensure that women stayed in the home, had babies, and did what they were told – and censured also by the many women who obeyed the rules, however much they disliked them, and did not want other women to rebel against something that they had learned to endure.*

"Who blames me?" Jane asks. "Many no doubt; and I shall be called discontented. I could not help it: the restlessness was in my nature; it agitated me to pain sometimes."

Life for most women in the 18th and early 19th centuries was not free, in the sense that we understand it today: choices were made *for* them, not *by* them.

"Then my sole relief," Jane continues, "was to walk along the corridor of the third story...safe in the silence and solitude of the spot, and allow my mind's eye to dwell on whatever bright visions rose before it – and certainly there were many and glowing; to let my heart be heaved by the exultant movement which, while it swelled it in trouble, expanded it with life; and best of all, to open my inward ear to a tale that never ended – a tale my imagination created, and narrated continuously; quickened with all of incident, life, fire, feeling, that I desired and had not in my actual existence."

Jane's desire for experience is so powerful that it becomes almost hallucinatory – it is a vision of a world full of passion, incident, and progress – an artistic vision belonging to Charlotte Bronte herself, who was confined in her small village, yearning for more *life*. But for most (especially poorer) women in the pre- and then Victorian era, existence was a narrow path indeed, and there were no exits until death.

Jane expands and amplifies her inner, personal ethos to include *all* women, defining a feminist vision well before its time:

"It is in vain to say human beings ought to be satisfied with tranquillity: they must have action; and they will make it if they cannot find it. Millions are condemned to a stiller doom than mine, and millions are in revolt against their silent lot. Nobody knows how many rebellions besides political rebellions ferment in the masses of life which people earth. Women are supposed to be very calm generally: but women feel just as men feel; they need exercise for their faculties, and a field for their efforts as much as their brothers do; they suffer from too rigid a restraint, too absolute a stagnation, precisely as men would suffer; and it is narrow-minded in their more privileged fellow creatures to say that they ought to confine themselves to making puddings and knitting stockings, to playing on the piano and embroidering bags. It is thoughtless to condemn them, or laugh at them, if they seek to do more or learn more than custom has pronounced necessary for their sex."

This section may well have been a response to Mary Wolstonecroft's book of 1792, *A Vindication of the Rights of Woman*, which was inspired by the principles of the French Revolution of 1789, and which argued for all women to receive a proper education and equal rights to men; it is often called the first published declaration of feminism. Charlotte Bronte valued it greatly.

ENTER EDWARD FAIRFAX ROCHESTER

In January of the new year, while Jane is taking a letter to be posted at the village of Hay, she encounters Rochester, whose horse stumbles and brings him down with it; Jane offers her assistance to help him remount. She is immediately struck by his physical presence:

"I could see him plainly. ...of middle height, and considerable breadth of chest. He had a dark face, with stern features and a heavy brow; his eyes and gathered eyebrows looked ireful and thwarted just now; he was past youth, but had not reached middle age; perhaps he might be thirty-five. I felt no fear of him, and but little shyness. Had he been a handsome, heroic-looking gentleman, I should not have dared to stand thus questioning him against his will, and offering my services unasked. I had hardly ever seen a handsome youth; never in my life spoken to one. I had a theoretical reverence and homage for beauty, elegance, gallantry, fascination; but had I met those qualities incarnate in masculine shape, I should have known instinctively that they neither had nor could have sympathy with anything in me..."

It is Rochester's unusual appearance that draws Jane, and she immediately feels an attraction to him that would have been impossible for her if he had been conventionally handsome - because someone like that could never have had any "sympathy" (she supposes) with someone so ordinary-looking as herself. Jane has little confidence in her exterior, and she has never yet met someone whose mind matches her own.

Rochester enlists her help, and Jane thinks, "I should have been afraid to touch a horse when alone, but when told to do it, I was disposed to obey."

When told to do it, I was disposed to obey. These few words, which flicker in the mind's eye, seeming to have little weight or permanence, actually contain the main directive in Jane's world up to that point. Jane's soul, her essence, has been in a towering struggle with the outside world since she was an infant in the care of Mrs Reed, fighting against what she sees as unfairness and injustice. All her young life, Jane has been "disposed to obey" - she has had no other option because she has had no power to set her own rules; whenever she has rebelled against injustice, she has been punished for it, and when rebellion is futile, autonomy is impossible. Jane has lived her life at the behest of those who wield power over her, but that era is ending: from now on, she will not feel the need to obey anybody without first questioning whether it is right. It is her relationship with Rochester that gives her this confidence, because it is the first time she will be treated (eventually) as an equal, and although he has all the power at the beginning of their relationship, by the time they marry, it is Jane who is in charge. The tumultuous campaign for independence which runs through the story is concluded near the end of the book in one sentence, on her reunion with Rochester, when Jane tells him proudly: "I am my own mistress."

From the moment of their first meeting, Jane is impressed by Rochester's physiognomy: "The new face...was like a new picture introduced to the gallery of memory...it was masculine...it was dark, strong, and stern." The sight of Rochester has awakened something dormant in Jane, a feeling unknown to her before. It is attraction, which is the beginning of love.

Jane returns to Thornfield still ignorant that Rochester is its owner. "I did not like re-entering Thornfield," she thinks. "To pass its threshold was to return to stagnation...an existence whose very privileges of security and ease I was becoming incapable of appreciating. What good it would have done me at that time to have been tossed in the storms of an uncertain struggling life, and to have been taught by rough and bitter experience to long for the calm amidst which I now repined!" This passage foreshadows the future: Jane *does* leave Thornfield and its comforts, and is compelled to go through extreme deprivation before she finds sanctuary.

Rochester now appears at the house and Jane learns that he is the owner; and this is where Jane's real life - the life she has been wishing and waiting for, the life of limitless possibility - begins.

Chapter 13

STAGE FOUR: ROCHESTER AND JANE FALL IN LOVE

Jane "discerned that Thornfield Hall was a changed place...a rill from the outer world was flowing through it; it had a master; for my part, I liked it better."

Rochester is not without physical faults, but Jane is clearly fascinated by his look and physique and is impelled to describe it in minute detail:

"...his broad and jetty eyebrows; his square forehead, made squarer by the horizontal sweep of his black hair. I recognised his decisive nose, more remarkable for character than beauty; his full nostrils, denoting, I thought, choler; his grim mouth, chin, and jaw - yes, all three were very grim, and no mistake. His shape, now divested of cloak, I perceived harmonized in squareness with his physiognomy: I suppose it was a good figure in the athletic sense of the term - broad chested and thin flanked; though neither tall nor graceful."

Rochester's tone towards other people is "impatient yet formal"; he is impatient because he thinks he knows more than everyone else (his position allows him to believe that), and he is formal because that is how he keeps people at a distance (with irony and excessive politeness). He feels, in other words, *vulnerable*, so he does his best to protect himself with verbal armour – but that armour is fragile before Jane, because she has an equally powerful intellect.

From the moment they meet, they begin their verbal jousting:

Rochester: "...did you expect a present, Miss Eyre?"
Jane: "I hardly know, sir; I have little experience of them: they are generally thought pleasant things."

Jane's tone is equally formal and ironic. She does not give him an inch.

Rochester compliments Jane on Adele's progress. Jane replies to Rochester as an intellectual equal and answers his rather intrusive questions with aplomb. By the tone of equality they adopt with each other, Bronte is indicating their suitability right from the start.

Rochester tells Mrs Fairfax that Jane was responsible for felling his horse: "I have to thank her for this sprain." He teases Jane about her looks, her schooling, her limited experience of life, but he is also watching her and noting her responses and her manner. Rochester takes liberties with someone he still does not know well, but the point is that Jane is not offended in the least, and he quickly comes to admire Jane for her strength of character. He is also impressed by Jane's drawings and asks her where they come from:

"Out of my head."
"That head I see now on your shoulders?"
"Yes, sir."
"Has it other furniture of the same kind within?"
"I should think it may have: I should hope – better."

Jane's drawings demonstrate a magical, mystical inventiveness. It is hard at first to imagine that these artworks come from the same mind as the self-deprecatory comments she makes about her looks – but then (as noted earlier) Jane has been living two lives up to now: the one, where her imagination soars without restraint, painting pictures in her mind that she admits are "but a pale portrait of the thing I had conceived" on paper; the other, where she is held back by the limits of her perception of herself. She shares with the reader some examples of the fantastical imagery she can conjure up onto paper:

"...a half-submerged mast...a cormorant, dark and large, with wings flecked with foam...its beak held a gold bracelet, set with gems...a drowned corpse glanced through the green water...the pinnacle of an iceberg piercing a polar winter sky...a colossal head...a brow quite bloodless, white as bone, and an eye hollow and fixed, blank of meaning but for the glassiness of despair...a ring of white flame, gemmed with sparkles of a more lurid tinge...the shape which shape had none..."

Jane inner life is exciting, exotic, full of mystery and wonder, the very opposite of her outer environment. Her imagination fills her with the delight lacking in her daily life, and she tells Rochester that painting what she is able to imagine is "one of the keenest pleasures I have ever known".

Later, Mrs Fairfax explains to Jane that there was discord in Rochester's family between him (Edward), his brother (Rowland), and his father. Mrs Fairfax knows only that Rochester was put in "a painful position...he broke with his family..." After his father's death, the death of his brother without a Will meant that Rochester inherited the whole estate, but Mrs Fairfax tells Jane that he spends very little time there. When Jane asks why, she is told that "perhaps he thinks it gloomy", which Jane considers an "evasive" answer.

There is more to Rochester's story, much more, and Jane senses it. But Mrs Fairfax is, it seems, ignorant of the mystery of the house's secret inhabitant.

Chapter 14

At first, Rochester pays little attention to Jane; there is "an occasional rencontre in the hall"; he addresses her "haughtily and coldly" with "a distant nod or cool glance" and a "rather sarcastic voice". Is this his customary way with new people, or is he playing a particular game with Jane? As he confesses much later, he was, even to the extent of toying with her. His plan is not even fully formed at this stage, and he has not yet decided whether to seduce her or fall in love with her. But he enjoyed the game. Should we censure such behaviour, the behaviour of a man much experienced in the world who was no stranger to seduction? Whether we do or not, Jane's personality, her combination of intelligence and honesty, disarms him; instead of an uncomplicated seduction – his initial preference, one feels sure – Rochester discovers that *he* is falling for *her.*

As for Jane, perhaps surprisingly, given her resistance to being dominated, she is immediately taken with Rochester's imperious demeanour: "Mr Rochester had such a direct way of giving orders, it seemed a matter of course to obey him promptly." And she continues to praise his features to herself, noting that he has "great, dark eyes…and very fine eyes, too".

On the other hand, she makes no attempt to flatter him:

"You examine me, Miss Eyre…do you think me handsome?"
"No, Sir."

Nor does he, her:

"You look very puzzled, Miss Eyre; and though you are not pretty any more than I am handsome, yet a puzzled air becomes you…"

And it is Jane's very directness, her lack of subterfuge or coquettishness that begins to win his respect:

"Ah! By my word! There is something singular about you…you have the air of a little nonnette; quaint, quiet, grave, and simple…"

A "nonnette" is a novice nun. Rochester sees that she is an innocent, and, given that he has been sated (and eventually disgusted) with the worldly women he has known before, a novelty. At any rate, Jane's virginal aura (implying purity and reticence) makes him comfortable enough – there is no sexual tension, so he can let down his guard – to start revealing himself to her:

"No young lady, I am not a general philanthropist; but I bear a conscience…and, besides, I once had a kind of rude tenderness of heart. When I was as old as you, I was a feeling fellow enough; partial to the unfledged, unfostered, and unlucky; but fortune has knocked me about since…"

(This is classic misanthropic male talk. When he was young, Rochester felt sorry for those less fortunate; now that he is older – and disappointed with the reception the world has given him – he can only feel sorry for *himself*.)

In the previous chapter, Jane spent a whole paragraph describing Rochester's features in some detail, and now, only a few pages later, she is giving the reader further description. These passages are clearly Jane's way of basking in the attraction she feels for him.

"…his unusual breadth of chest, disproportionate almost to his length of limb. I am sure most people would have thought him an ugly man; yet there was so much unconscious pride in his port; so much ease in his demeanour; such a look of complete indifference to his external appearance; so haughty a reliance on the power of other qualities, intrinsic or adventitious, to atone for the lack of mere personal attractiveness, that in looking at him, one inevitably shared the indifference…"

Rochester begins to deal with Jane more like an acquaintance than an employee:

"I don't wish to treat you like an inferior…I claim only such superiority as must result from twenty years' difference in age and a century's advance in experience."

Jane, however, is not prepared to award him any implicit rights merely for his seniority:

"I don't think, sir, you have a right to command me, merely because you are older than I, or because you have seen more of the world…"

And:

"I was thinking, sir, that very few masters would trouble themselves to inquire whether or not their paid subordinates were piqued and hurt by their orders."

Perhaps Jane is beginning to realise that he is no longer looking at her as a governess, but as a woman. She too becomes more familiar with him – until she oversteps whatever invisible line Rochester has drawn on her presumption, and he puts her in her place again:

"...don't venture on generalities of which you are intensely ignorant..."

He continues:

"...if you are cast in a different mould to the majority, it is no merit of yours: Nature did it. ...you may have intolerable defects to counter-balance your few good points."

"And so may you," thinks Jane.

Jane has the last laugh and the best line. But this takes place in her head. She is not yet confident enough – or enough of a confidant – to make such an observation aloud.

Rochester slowly reveals his inner self, his turbulent interior, to Jane, while continuing to patronise her (he cannot yet bring himself to talk openly because he is still not sure if he can trust her):

"I have a past existence, a series of deeds, a colour of life to contemplate within my own breast, which might well call my sneers and censures from my neighbours to myself. I started, or rather...was thrust on to a wrong tack at the age of one and twenty, and have never recovered the right course since: but I might have been very different; I might have been as good as you, – wiser, – almost as stainless. I envy you your peace of mind, your clean conscience, your unpolluted memory. Little girl, a memory without blot of contamination must be an exquisite treasure...is it not?"

He adds:

"I was your equal at eighteen - quite your equal. Nature meant me to be, on the whole, a good man, Miss Eyre: one of the better end; and you see I am not so."

"I am not a villain...I am a trite common-place sinner, hackneyed in all the poor petty dissipations with which the rich and worthless try to put on life..."

These revelations coming from Rochester, albeit without specific details yet, show us that he begins to feel confident enough in Jane to unburden himself of the great mental weight he has been carrying around for years - the twin burdens of guilt and shame. Chapter 14 is the point at which Jane shows herself his mental and intellectual equal; it is, perhaps, the moment they fall in love, even if they do not know it quite yet.

Then the atmosphere changes and their relationship begins to develop some depth. Rochester ceases teasing Jane and starts to compliment her:

"Know that, in the course of your future life you will often find yourself elected the involuntary confidant of your acquaintances' secrets: people will instinctively find out, as I have done, that it is not your forte to talk of yourself, but to listen while others talk of themselves; they will feel, too, that you listen with no malevolent scorn of their indiscretions, but with a kind of infinite sympathy; not the less comforting and encouraging because it is very unobtrusive in its manifestations."

While Rochester talks of his regrets, Jane has been listening closely, and responds in a way that shows considerable confidence, even courage, given their inchoate (unformed, undefined) relationship:

"Only one thing I know: you said you were not as good as you should like to be, and that you regretted your own imperfection...It seems to me, that if you tried hard, you would in time find it possible to become what you yourself would approve; and that if from this day you began with resolution to correct your thoughts and actions, you would in a few years have laid up a new and stainless store of recollections, to which you might revert with pleasure."

Jane continues to instruct Rochester in a way that he cannot have experienced before. After all, who would dare to speak to him like this except for Jane? She is wise and perceptive - in spite of her naivety. Her precepts are powerful and come from her comfortless upbringing and from her understanding of the Bible. Rochester recognises this power in her and salutes it, for he says:

"I think you will learn to be natural with me, as I find it impossible to be conventional with you; and then your looks and movements will have more vivacity and variety than they dare offer now. I see, at intervals, the glance of a curious sort of bird through the close-set bars of a cage: a vivid, restless, resolute captive is there; were it but free, it would soar cloud-high."

For the first time in perhaps a very long while, Rochester feels relaxed enough to talk without affectation or obfuscation. Jane has already had a considerable and salutary effect on him.

Chapter 15

BERTHA ON THE ATTACK

Rochester, with increasing confidence in her, tells Jane about his time in Europe (omitting any mention of his time in the Caribbean - or of Bertha). He talks about the affair with Celine Varens, how she cheated on him with another man, and how he fought a duel with his rival (we are not told if he killed him). Adele is Celine's daughter; but whether she is also Rochester's, or another man's, is not revealed. In any case, Rochester took on the raising of the child as if it were his own.

"You never felt jealousy, did you, Miss Eyre? Of course not: I need not ask you; because you never felt love. You have both sentiments yet to experience: your soul sleeps; the shock is yet to be given which shall waken it." Jane is going to receive the "shock" soon enough.

And Rochester tells her: "I wish to be a better man than I have been; than I am..." The power of love is that it makes people want to be better versions of themselves; Rochester is falling for Jane and wants her to believe he can shake off the past and reform himself. As he then says:

"Strange that I should choose you for the confidant of all this, young lady: passing strange that you should listen to me quietly, as if it were the most usual thing in the world for a man like me to tell stories of his opera-mistresses to a quaint, inexperienced girl like you! But the last singularity explains the first, as I intimated once before: you, with your gravity, considerateness, and caution were made to be the recipient of secrets. Besides, I know what sort of a mind I have placed in communication with my own; I know it is one not liable to take infection: it is a peculiar mind; it is an unique one. ...The more you and I converse, the better; for while I cannot blight you, you may refresh me."

Jane also sees a change in Rochester, but she does not yet know (or dare to know) that it is love which makes him try harder to please her:

"His deportment had now for some weeks been more uniform towards me than at the first. I never seemed in his way; he did not take fits of chilling hauteur: when he met me unexpectedly, the encounter seemed welcome; he had always a word and sometimes a smile for me: when summoned by formal invitation to his presence, I was honoured by a cordiality of reception that made me feel I really possessed the power to amuse him, and that these evening conferences were sought as much for his pleasure as for my benefit."

And this convergence between the two of them continues:

"The ease of his manner freed me from painful restraint: the friendly frankness, as correct as cordial...drew me to him. I felt at times, as if he were my relation, rather than my master...I ceased to pine after kindred: my thin crescent-destiny seemed to enlarge; the blanks of existence were filled up; my bodily health improved; I gathered flesh and strength."

The above segment is especially interesting. Jane talks of her "thin crescent-destiny", of the "blanks of existence", and sums it up with "my bodily health improved". These phrases all hint at an internal emptiness, specifically an *enforced emptiness of body. A "thin crescent-destiny", with its singular image of a bowed form (crescent) resulting from a future that is "thin" brings to mind someone who is starving herself, her body bent by lack of food, and the implication that without a worthwhile future, there is no sense in eating; the "blanks" of existence - another form of emptiness, possibly an allusion to meals that were missed or uneaten. And now that Jane feels wanted by Rochester, she gathers "flesh and strength", and her "bodily health improved" - how else would her health improve unless she was eating properly again? In the next chapter, Jane tells us that she "now looked much better than I did", and that she now had "more colour and more flesh". More <u>flesh</u>? That is a word with no ambiguity. Jane is putting on weight.*

Is it possible, then - or, more likely, probable - that Jane had an eating disorder? And that Rochester unknowingly cured her of it? We remember something Jane said early on in the story, in Chapter 2, when she threatened "never eating or drinking more, and letting myself die." A brief line, easy to disregard as the emotional outburst of a child - and yet, in the light of her constant self-denigration on the subject of her looks, frequent references to her size (as small, little, frail, etc.) and the ambiguous comments she makes in this chapter, perhaps not a throwaway line at all, but an important and enduring statement of intent.

This theory may sound fanciful, but, then again, it has the resonance of truth. Bronte leaves clues for the reader to discover, if the reader is alert; and, what is more, because Jane is her creation, her very double in many ways, it is not an implausible leap to imagine that Bronte herself had "issues" with food.

Enough. Let us return to Jane's favourite subject. From this next segment we learn that, while Jane is now undoubtedly taken with Rochester, she holds back her complete approval because she sees him being hard on others (even if he has ceased being so hard on *her*). This is difficult for Jane to witness, because she deplores people who abuse their power, having suffered from similar treatment in the past:

"And was Mr Rochester now ugly in my eyes? No, reader, gratitude, and many associations, all pleasurable and genial, made his face the object I best liked to see; his presence in a room was more cheering than the brightest fire. Yet I had not forgotten his faults: indeed, I could not, for he brought them frequently before me. He was proud, sardonic, harsh to inferiority of every description: in my secret soul I knew that his great kindness to me was balanced by unjust severity to many others."

Jane is shrewd enough to perceive that there is a reason for Rochester's rough edges, but she does not yet know that it is the insoluble Bertha problem which continually chafes and causes him to overreact:

"...I believed that his moodiness, his harshness, and his former faults of morality (I say former, for now he seemed corrected of them) had their source in some cruel cross of fate. I believed he was naturally a man of better tendencies, higher principles, and purer tastes than such as circumstances had developed, education instilled, or destiny encouraged. I thought there were some excellent materials in him...I cannot deny that I grieved for his grief, whatever that was, and would have given much to assuage it."

At this point the author jolts us with the entrance of Bertha Mason (although we do not yet know it is she) when she escapes from her prison and tries to burn Rochester to death in his room by setting fire to the bed curtains. Fortunately, Jane is awoken by odd noises and rushes to Rochester's assistance – saving his life, no less. Afterwards, Rochester chooses not to tell her about Bertha, instead informing Jane that the responsible person was Grace Poole.

"You have saved my life," Rochester tells her. "I have a pleasure in owing you so immense a debt. I cannot say more. Nothing else that has being would have been tolerable to me in the character of creditor for such an obligation: but you; it is different; – I feel your benefits no burden, Jane."

This honest, sincere affirmation seems to come unprepared, perhaps because Rochester suddenly realises that Jane is the first person he has known who would come to his help without the expectation of a reward. He continues:

"I knew...you would do me some good in some way, at some time; – I saw it in your eyes when I first beheld you: their expression and smile did not...strike delight to my very inmost heart so for nothing. People talk of natural sympathies... My cherished preserver, goodnight!"

Jane retires to her room:

"Till morning dawned I was tossed on a buoyant but unquiet sea, where billows of trouble rolled under surges of joy. I thought I saw beyond its wild waters a shore...and now and then a freshening gale wakened by hope, bore my spirit triumphantly towards the bourne: but I could not reach it, even in fancy... Sense would resist delirium: judgment would warn passion."

Jane is in love, but with her there are always "sense" and "judgment" acting as twin anchors on her emotions, which would threaten to spiral out of control otherwise; Jane will be grateful for these twin anchors in the future, given what happens to her hopes of happiness.

VOL. II

Chapter 16

Next day, the story is that Rochester himself extinguished the fire, which was caused by a candle. Jane quizzes Grace Poole; there is no evidence that she is the culprit, although Grace asks questions of Jane to see how much *she* knows. Jane is perplexed by Grace's presence and role at Thornfield - and why she has not been taken into custody, if she was responsible for the fire of the previous night. Jane wonders if Grace does not have some power over Rochester - perhaps even that he has committed an "indiscretion" with her. Jane cannot believe Rochester would be attracted to the rough-looking Grace, but, then, she also cannot believe that Rochester has taken a liking to *her*, although she is beginning to recognise the probability that he has, even as she dismisses the idea of Grace:

"No; impossible! My supposition cannot be correct. Yet ...you are not beautiful, either, and perhaps Mr Rochester approves you: at any rate you have often felt as if he did; and last night – remember his words; remember his look; remember his voice!"

Jane mentioned in the previous chapter that she considered Rochester to have been "corrected" of his "former faults of morality", yet here she finds it possible to imagine him having an affair with Grace Poole. Does that reflect a lack of faith in her judgment – or in Rochester?

"I hastened to drive from my mind the hateful notion I had been conceiving regarding Grace Poole: it disgusted me. I compared myself with her, and found we were different. …I was a lady. And now I looked much better than I did…I had more colour and more flesh; more life, more vivacity; because I had brighter hopes and keener enjoyment."

Jane longs to talk to Rochester about the recent strange events, and the next passage reveals just how much confidence Jane now has in her dealings with him. At the beginning of their acquaintance we know that Rochester enjoyed teasing – even taunting – her; now Jane reveals that she is giving him much the same treatment:

"I knew the pleasure of vexing and soothing him by turns; it was one I chiefly delighted in, and a sure instinct always prevented me from going too far: beyond the verge of provocation I never ventured; on the extreme brink I liked to try my skill. Retaining every minute form of respect, every propriety of my station, I could still meet him in argument without fear or uneasy restraint: this suited both him and me."

At this point in the story, Bronte wisely takes the focus away from Rochester's and Jane's relationship, in order to give them (and us) some breathing space, and transports him away from Thornfield to visit his neighbours, a group of local ladies and gentlemen, "fine, fashionable people", according to Mrs Fairfax. Amongst them is the Ingram family, and one Blanche Ingram, whom Mrs Fairfax calls "the queen". Blanche will become Jane's competition for Rochester. We learn that "Mr Rochester is near forty", and Blanche is twenty-five. Jane wants to know more, as we always do about the competition. Alone again, Jane resolves to quell those feelings of hope and desire for Rochester which threaten to become unmanageable: he is out of your league, she reminds herself. And, as is customary with Jane, when feeling vulnerable, she turns her insecurity against herself. Persons of a sensitive nature may want to skip over the next few examples, which show just how relentlessly negative Jane can become when uncertain of her future:

"...a greater fool than Jane Eyre had never breathed the breath of life...a more fantastic idiot had never surfeited herself on sweet lies, and swallowed poison as if it were nectar."

"You...a favourite with Mr Rochester? You gifted with the power of pleasing him? You of importance to him in any way? Go! Your folly sickens me."

Jane tells herself to look in the mirror: "'Portrait of a Governess, disconnected, poor, and plain.'"

And having successfully convinced herself yet again that she is worthless and insignificant – and ugly – Jane corrects her future course away from the danger of amorous rapture and back to self-control:

"Order! No snivel! – no sentiment! – no regret! I will endure only sense and resolution."

And she offers some sensible advice to every woman:

"It does good to no woman to be flattered by her superior, who cannot intend to marry her; and it is madness in all women to let a secret love kindle within them, which, if unreturned and unknown, must devour the life that feeds it; and, if discovered and responded to, must lead, ignis-fatuus-like, into miry wilds whence there is no extrication."

Jane decides to paint an imaginary portrait of Blanche Ingram (whom she has not yet seen) in the role of "an accomplished lady of rank". She later does the same thing with Rosamond Oliver, the young woman with whom St John Rivers is in love. The exercise appears to be a way of putting herself in her place (the place she is trying to escape from, the place of inferiority), and reminding herself not to be hopeful, because she intends, having painted the portrait of Blanche, to place it next to a mirror and sit in front of it, imagining Rochester's reaction:

"…take out these two pictures and compare them: say…is it likely he would waste a serious thought on this indigent and insignificant plebean?"

Referring to herself uncompromisingly as "plebean" (common), as well as "indigent" (dirt poor) and "insignificant" in one breath is quite extraordinary, given what has been occurring between her and Rochester, as if all her recent meetings, discussions, and the feelings passing between them have been erased in an instant. At the first sign of a serious obstacle, Jane knocks herself back down to the floor – again.

Yet the finished portrait, while allowing Jane to indulge the innate sense of inadequacy that haunts her, also provides some relief from it:

" 'Ere long, I had reason to congratulate myself on the course of wholesome discipline to which I had thus forced my feelings to submit: thanks to it, I was able to meet subsequent occurrences with a decent calm; which, had they found me unprepared, I should probably have been unequal to maintain, even externally."

A roundabout way of saying that if she had not driven jealousy of Blanche out of her heart by setting her down on paper, and somehow limiting the harmful effect by doing so, the thought of Blanche - the possibility of Blanche with Rochester - might have been too much to bear.

Rochester's earlier warning to Jane about the "shock" she would experience when at last she fell in love and became jealous over the object of her love was only too prophetic.

Chapter 17

Rochester is away for ten days. Mrs Fairfax further disquiets Jane by saying he might have left the country. "When I heard this I was beginning to feel a strange chill and failing at the heart. …a sickening sense of disappointment…" Jane "at once called [her] sensations to order"; a young, intelligent woman in the 19th century was taught to exert control over her emotions, however painful. It was unladylike to do otherwise.

Jane reminds herself (again) that she has no rights over Rochester and advises herself: "…don't make him the object of your fine feelings, your raptures, agonies, and so forth. He is not of your order: keep to your caste; and be too self-respecting to lavish the love of the whole heart, soul, and strength, where such a gift is not wanted and would be despised." Once more doubting herself, Jane attacks herself; and yet, even while doing this, there is a sense that she continues to hold out hope.

Our heroine does not consider herself worthy of the object of her affections, does not dare to hope he might want her: she is a working girl, he is a gentleman, etc. (The script is not unlike many rom-com films.) And yet, while Jane tortures herself in a frenzy of hope and self-hatred, Rochester, oblivious of the agonies she is undergoing, is calmly falling in love with her.

Jane continues to struggle with her thoughts and is "in spite of myself, thrown back on the region of doubts and portents, and dark conjectures…" She knows something is amiss at Thornfield, but what that is, she cannot yet identify. She overhears two servants talking about Grace Poole and revealing that she is paid a lot more than they are. They might know something – but they cease their chatter as soon as Jane approaches. "All I had gathered from it amounted to this," Jane thinks, "– there was a mystery at Thornfield; and that from participation in that mystery, I was purposely excluded."

News arrives that Rochester is returning with guests. The house must be made ready. When they arrive, Jane is instantly intimidated by their "high-born elegance". From upstairs that night she can overhear their celebrations and next day witnesses Rochester and Blanche Ingram riding out - together. Jane is crushed, although she keeps it hidden from Mrs Fairfax. Rochester requests her and Adele's presence after dinner in the main salon.

From her place in the salon, Jane watches the guests' entry into the drawing-room: "some of them were very tall" (Jane is petite, as we know), and displayed a "sweeping amplitude of array" (Jane is modestly dressed); their whole mien (bearing, manner) is of insouciant (casual, careless) and accustomed entitlement (they "threw themselves in half-reclining positions on the sofa"). The three "most distinguished" to Jane are the Dowager Lady Ingram (with "an expression of almost insupportable haughtiness") and her daughters, Blanche ("moulded like a Dian" - the goddess Diana) and Mary. Jane mentions Blanche's "arched and haughty lip" and that she is "remarkably self-conscious indeed".

Rochester enters the room, and Jane reminds herself of their recent closeness after she saved him from being burned alive. "How near I had approached him at that moment!" she thinks, regretting their separation. Now she feels cut off from him by the splendour of his guests: "…how distant, how far estranged we were!" Jane stares at him ("my eyes were drawn involuntarily to his face: I could not keep their lids under control…"), and while mentally listing his prominent features *again* ("not beautiful, according to rule"), she also adds that "they were more than beautiful to me: they were full of an interest, an influence that quite mastered me, - that took my feelings from my own power and fettered them in his."

Power, mastery, influence: before Rochester came into her life, only God had such sway over her. This is an important time for Jane: it marks her transition from the world of the imagination (religion and art) to the "real" world (of human love and human relationships). It is interesting that once her future is secure with Rochester (at the end of the book), we hear no more of her drawing - her imagination goes into hibernation as her "real" life begins.

"I had not intended to love him."

This is Jane's first real and outward confession of her love for Rochester. Yes, "the reader knows I had wrought hard to extirpate from my soul the germs of love there detected; and now, at the first renewed view of him, they spontaneously revived, green and strong! He made me love him without looking at me."

Bronte writes persuasively of the effects of love: *he made me love him without looking at me.* How undeniably true that is: we've all suffered from it. Some would say that *not* seeing the object of one's love is as – or *more* – potent than actually looking at it. The imagination does its work in amplifying and enlarging the idea of the loved one while he or she is unseen, and Jane has had ten days to think about nothing but Rochester while he has been away; she has created a whole spectrum of desire, a rainbow of feeling, in her mind.

That Bronte frequently uses the words "master" and "mastered" in a story that has proved so popular with women over nearly two centuries seems to indicate that the theme of dominance is an attractive element to readers. But what makes *Jane Eyre* so original (and ahead of its time) is Jane's strength of character, for while she uses these words so frequently that the reader must assume she enjoys the usage – the sensation of someone controlling her in a pleasing way – Jane is never submissive or subservient: she questions everything.

We listen in as the Ingrams discuss "governesses" – with pointed reference to Jane sitting nearby – and the comments are (of course) defamatory on the subject. Lady Ingram is heard to say, referring to Jane, that she sees in her "all the faults of her class". Blanche calls "the whole tribe" a "nuisance", then summons Rochester to the piano for songs, flirting with him flamboyantly and complimenting his look ("a man is nothing without a spice of the devil in him"). Rochester trades compliments with her, all the while aware that Jane is overhearing what he says. This is cruel, no doubt about it, and is all part of his plan to subdue her will – at this stage he still has not decided whether he should seduce Jane or marry her; but it is Rochester who is subdued in the end, and Jane who is triumphant.

But at this moment, an embattled Jane, dismayed by everything happening around her, makes to leave the room – and encounters Rochester on the way out; he inquires after her health and ends with "Goodnight, my –"

...Love?

Chapter 18

STRANGE GAMES AT THORNFIELD

The guests take over Thornfield: "there was life everywhere, movement all day long..."

Proposing a game of charades, Lady Ingram says Jane "looks too stupid for any game of the sort." We witness Rochester and Blanche in costume, looking every inch the imperial couple in their roles. Jane cannot take her eyes from the spectacle of Rochester behaving intimately with her; she recalls, even as she is writing the story, "their interchanged glances; and something even of the feeling roused by the spectacle returns in memory at this moment." Now happily married to Rochester, the pangs of envy and jealousy she felt then are still painfully recalled. Such sensations are impossible to erase, no matter the distance in time.

"I have told you, reader," Jane confides to us miserably, "that I had learnt to love Mr Rochester: I could not unlove him now, merely because I found that he had ceased to notice me...I could not unlove him, because I felt sure he would soon marry this very lady..."

In spite of her suffering (or perhaps because of it), Jane still finds composure enough to deride Blanche in considerable detail: "She was very showy, but she was not genuine"; "...her mind was poor, her heart barren by nature"; "She was not good; she was not original"; "...she did not know the sensations of sympathy and pity; tenderness and truth were not in her..." (It is a fact, and a sad one, that we humans tend to attack anybody with whom we feel inadequate by comparison.)

Jane watches Rochester closely, sees him recoil inwardly at Blanche's behaviour, and such is Jane's connection to him that even though he clearly does not desire Blanche, *this* upsets her, too: "...the future bridegroom, Mr Rochester himself, exercised over his intended a ceaseless surveillance: and it was from this sagacity - this guardedness of his - his perfect, clear consciousness of his fair one's defects - this obvious absence of passion in his sentiments towards her, that my ever-torturing pain arose."

Jane sees that "he was going to marry her, for family, perhaps political reasons; because her rank and connexions suited him; I felt he had not given her his love, and that her qualifications were ill adapted to win from him that treasure. This was the point – this was where the nerve was touched and teased – this was where the fever was sustained and fed: *she could not charm him*."

Jane observes; she ruminates; she comments. She is as unsparing in her assessment of Blanche as she is of herself. What she sees is that for all Blanche's efforts to seduce Rochester, he is not falling for her wiles. This puts Jane "under ceaseless excitation and ruthless restraint" – she is being pulled apart, seeing how Blanche "might have succeeded." "It seems to me," Jane conjectures, "that she might, by merely sitting quietly at his side, saying little and looking less, get nigher his heart". (nigher = nearer to)

Jane cannot imagine how Blanche will please him when they are married – but *she* knows how. And while Jane would never marry for anything less than love, she understands with all the clarity of an outsider how class and society put pressure on people like Rochester and Blanche to conform.

Meanwhile, Jane finds herself "growing very lenient" towards Rochester's faults. "Now I saw no bad", she states. The "sarcasm" and "harshness" that had upset her in the beginning are now no more than "keen condiments in a choice dish". (When even his worst faults seem attractive to her, she must indeed be head over heels.)

Now there is the unexpected arrival of Richard Mason (Bertha's brother, unknown as such yet); to Jane, there is something odd and vacant about him: "his eye wandered, and had no meaning in its wandering." She does not like his look, although the other ladies find him appealing. He talks of the West Indies, and Jane learns that Rochester was living out there.

Another surprise follows: a gypsy woman arrives at the house to tell the guests' fortunes. (It is Rochester in drag.) Why does he do this? It appears that his intention is to tell Blanche's future and put her off marrying him by saying that he has no money – the most effective way, in his mind, to rid himself of her. It would have been more courteous, more gentlemanly, if he had told Blanche in person that he had no intention of marrying her, but, as we are beginning to realise, Rochester's unhappiest flaw is his refusal to take responsibility for himself. Anyway, the ruse works: Blanche emerges from the interview "dissatisfied" and her face "sourly expressive of disappointment". Gypsy Rochester has not given her glad tidings. Jane is now summoned for an interview.

Chapter 19

There follows a most curious scene between Rochester and Jane. Rochester the gypsy lists Jane's faults to her: "You are cold; you are sick; and you are silly." What, exactly, is Rochester playing at here? It appears to be another step in his campaign to win her by disparaging her, breaking down her defences so that she will be more easily managed. (Rochester admires her resistance, but prefers her compliance.) By saying what he wants to say in disguise, he can avoid feeling guilty for his underhand actions. Curious behaviour, indeed, but we should remember that his experiences with women have been, to say the least, problematic, and he has become exceedingly wary of being himself, even though his instincts tell him to trust Jane.

He goes on to tell Jane that she is "very near happiness...within reach of it." All that is required is "a movement"; but why should it be *Jane* who moves – why not he, Rochester? Because he has a secret which he is terrified of divulging: he's *married*, and, in the back of his mind and scarcely unacknowledged even to himself, he would like to seduce Jane without telling her anything about Bertha beforehand. If Jane were to make a move on *him* rather than the other way round, he could feel less guilty about his deception (and be able to blame her for seducing him when his secret came out, as it would, eventually). The problem for Rochester is that Jane is far too cautious and clever for him: she just won't swoon into his arms without keeping at least one eye open for trickery. He is still underestimating her.

Gypsy Rochester continues to test Jane to see at what stage of infatuation for him she currently stands; he asks her if she has "some secret hope" – he wants to hear that she is crazy about him, then he can manipulate her more easily – but Jane is reticent about answering (and wisely, too). Indeed, Jane reveals that she considers marriage a "catastrophe". (She is right in one sense – it *will* be a catastrophe when she discovers that Rochester is already married – and on her wedding day to him, as well.)

Rochester continues to probe Jane for proof that she loves him – and she continues to avoid giving an answer. "You have seen love: have you not?" he asks Jane, who is obliged to admit her suspicion that Rochester will be married to Miss Ingram. Here the gypsy implies that all is not entirely settled between them, but Jane does not ask for more information. Again the gypsy tells Jane that it is up to her to "stretch out" her hand and take up her fortune (another blatant attempt to get her to make the first move). All this devious, tortuous manoeuvring provides Rochester with cover while he tries to seduce Jane, but it does not excuse him from wooing her at all while Bertha inhabits the upstairs, however victimised he may feel.

Rochester follows up with a comprehensive analysis of Jane's personality, based on her physiognomy. If he's so sure he has Jane all worked out, why doesn't he trust her enough to tell her that he is married? Because he *doesn't* really trust her – but, what is worse, he doesn't trust *himself* with her. At last, Rochester tires of the game and obliquely reveals his true identity to Jane. She is not terribly amused – and who would be?

Jane tells Rochester that Mason has arrived at the house, and his response is swift and direct (no obscurity this time): "Jane, I've got a blow; – I've got a blow, Jane!" He is strongly affected by this unwelcome news – and holds Jane's hand for support. He tells Jane to see how Mason is behaving; she returns to tell him that there is nothing amiss in the drawing-room. Mason has not told the party about Bertha, then, or there would have been an uproar. Rochester asks Jane to tell Mason to go to him.

Chapter 20

BERTHA MAKES HER ENTRANCE (OFFSTAGE)

That night, Jane is awoken by a terrible scream coming from the room above her (Bertha's – and we might ask why Rochester has allowed Jane to reside in such close proximity, it's asking for trouble).

The entire house is jolted to attention: the guests all come out of their rooms and Rochester must allay their fears with an improbable tale of a servant having a nightmare. Jane is summoned to assist him. Rochester takes Jane's hand (by degrees, their intimacy grows more physical). Rochester shows her the secret room behind the curtain (but he does not open it). "A snarling, snatching sound" issues forth. In the outer room, Mason has been badly mauled and is lying on the bed. Jane still believes Grace Poole is the culprit.

Jane is troubled by the events she has experienced. "What mystery, that broke out, now in fire and now in blood, at the deadliest hours of night? - what creature was it, that, masked in an ordinary women's face and shape, uttered the voice, now of a mocking demon, and anon of a carrion-seeking bird of prey?" (Bronte channelling some Gothic horror imagery, no doubt with an eye to future readers.)

Jane tries to understand the relationship between Rochester and Mason, and why Rochester has been so disconcerted by Mason's arrival, especially as Mason seems so entirely under his control.

Rochester, instructing Jane to keep watch over Mason, disappears from the room; Jane has to remain and nurse Mason for hours until Rochester returns with the doctor, Carter, who is told to patch up Mason with all speed, because Rochester wants him off the premises by sunrise. "She sucked the blood," Mason says; "she said she'd drain my heart...." (More Gothic nonsense.) Rochester repeats that Mason must leave urgently; "I have striven long to avoid exposure", he says, "and I should not like it to come at last." Why Mason has said nothing to Jane about Bertha while he was lying semi-delirious on the bed is curious, but for the sake of the plot, understandable. Even more curious is Jane's lack of enquiry concerning the creature behind the door; we must assume that her love for Rochester will not allow her to probe him further on the matter - even though, being no fool, Jane knows something serious is being kept from her.

Early the next morning, after the doctor has finished his handiwork, Mason is hustled out of the house and into a post-chaise waiting for him. Mason breaks into tears as they part: "Let her be taken care of..." he implores Rochester. (Why he has never suggested to

Rochester that they find some real medical help for Bertha is inexplicable – he is her *brother*, after all.)

Rochester asks Jane to walk with him. He comments on the purity of nature compared with the corruption inside the house. Jane, of course, does not understand his true meaning – yet. Rochester offers her a flower. He calls her his "pet lamb"(the reader may be forgiven for finding it rather distasteful that Rochester continues to woo Jane while Bertha is still rampaging a few floors above ground). And we must feel considerable pity for Jane – who has been up all night and still believes that it is Grace Poole inside the hidden room – when Rochester starts making ominous declarations: "To live, for me, Jane, is to stand on a crater-crust which may crack and spew fire any day." Jane remains wilfully innocent of the true nature of the incident in which she has just participated, and she does not press Rochester for answers, as if she already knows that the truth will compel her to leave him. Rochester is very aware of this fact, and the tone he employs now is both impatient and frustrated: he wants to keep the secret safe but he also wants to be rid of it. "Well, you too have power over me, and may injure me," he says to Jane, continuing, "I dare not show you where I am vulnerable, lest, faithful and friendly as you are, you should transfix me at once." He is afraid of telling the truth; and when a man is afraid of being found out by someone who loves him, he is not taking responsibility for himself, or being fair to the other person.

There is something sinister in Rochester's method: he recognises his power over Jane and he toys with her while still inching towards his goal of taking her as his wife – or mistress (all without having to reveal his secret). He insinuates that he has been unlucky, if not ill-treated, and, by acting like the victim in the matter, he inveigles Jane to help him. But the truth is not as simple as Rochester would wish (and he knows it). After all, who is the *real* victim here? Rochester – or Bertha?

Rochester talks about himself as if entirely removed from his past, as "a wild boy" in his youth, and later as an unfortunate bystander who seems, through no fault of his own, to have been implicated in an unpleasant accident – marrying Bertha. He tells Jane that he has committed "a capital error", but not a crime. An "*error*" (his italics);

but was it not a *crime* (my italics) to lock up Bertha? He says, ambiguously, that what he took were "unusual measures, but neither unlawful nor culpable"; but, again, is it *lawful* to lock up one's wife? Is that not very *culpable*? Not to Rochester, clearly, in the early 1800s. He pities himself - and wants Jane to pity him, too. But he will not reveal the truth.

Then he tells Jane that since he met her, her society "revives, regenerates" him; he has "higher wishes, purer feelings"; he wants to "recommence" his life "in a way more worthy of an immortal being" (meaning his soul - which he hopes Jane will cleanse with her stainless purity). Then, in a way that Jane could not possibly grasp the meaning of, he talks about "overleaping an obstacle of custom", i.e., taking Jane as his wife/lover while Bertha is still alive. He claims his conscience is clear and his judgment sound. Really?

Jane tries to glean more detail, which he won't give, so she refers him to God for guidance. Rochester, now despairing of imparting his meaning to Jane (but still unwilling to come clean, because she would run a mile), says that he has been "a worldly, dissipated, restless man", but that "I believe I have found the instrument for my cure..." Here he breaks off without coming to the final point: *Jane* is his cure. He does not see it as *his* responsibility to purge his conscience by admitting what he has done, asking forgiveness, rectifying the situation - no, it is up to *Jane* to save him. What a fine man, indeed.

Having emptied himself out of complaints while still not coming to the heart of the matter - and realising Jane is not to be goaded any longer without pushing back - Rochester again goes into silent mode; his tone reverts to the old sulky Rochester, "becoming harsh and sarcastic" - the pendulum has swung the other way again. He clasps Jane's hand; he invites her to "sit up with me", supposedly the night before his marriage - to Blanche! He even has the nerve to ask Jane whether she finds Blanche seductive. "She's a rare one, is she not, Jane?" Clearly he *enjoys* taunting her, knowing that Jane is in love with him (but he is also in love with *her*, so he is also hurting himself - and enjoying the pain, presumably, because he has been behaving like this for some time). One thing that binds Jane and Rochester - and Bronte - together is their tripartite tendency towards self-inflicted hurt.

Chapter 21

MRS REED REQUESTS JANE'S PRESENCE

The next day, Jane receives a visit from Leaven, the coachman from Gateshead. He reports that Mrs Reed's son, John – the bully from Jane's childhood – is dead; he borrowed heavily from his mother ("his life has been very wild", Leaven says), and now Mrs Reed herself is lying ill after a stroke and has asked for Jane. Jane requests leave from Rochester, who has heard of the Reeds, describing John as "one of the veriest rascals in town" and Georgiana as "much admired for her beauty". Rochester does not want her gone for more than a week, and when Jane demurs, insists that she must return to him as soon as possible.

Jane, who continues to believe that Rochester will marry Blanche, tells him that after the marriage Adele should be sent away to school and that she should seek "another situation elsewhere". Rochester is clearly dismayed by this news and obliges Jane to trust him to find her a new situation (he means as his wife). Jane insists that she must be gone before his bride comes to live at Thornfield. Their parting is unsatisfactory: Jane wants to go quickly, Rochester wants her to say more than a mere "farewell" – he would have enjoyed it if she had broken down and told him how much she was going to miss him; but she is stronger than that. And then *he* suddenly departs, as if Jane has hurt him, even though he knows he is hurting her. There is, however, no way that Rochester will tell Jane the truth about his past (Bertha) or his present (Blanche) until he is sure he has her in his complete power and can control her – but Jane will not abase herself before him, and this failure to bow down on her part puts him in a foul temper. For the time being, it is stalemate between them.

Jane takes the coach and arrives at Gateshead lodge the next day. Bessie the servant is happy to see her. "I knew you would come!" she says. Jane tells Bessie that Rochester is "rather an ugly man, but quite a gentleman"; this odd revelation to a comparative stranger indicates how hurt Jane is at the thought of his impending marriage. They talk, and then Jane continues to "the same hostile roof" that she knew before.

"I had yet an aching heart. I still felt like a wanderer on the face of the earth; but I experienced firmer trust in myself and my own powers, and less withering dread of oppression. The gaping wound of my wrongs, too, was now quite healed; and the flame of resentment extinguished." This important passage shows how Jane has matured in the years since she lived at Gateshead, and how she has learned to control her powerful urge for retaliation and requital.

The two daughters are there: Eliza, thin, sallow, severe, "nun-like", and Georgiana: plump, stylish, but with her mother's "contour of jaw and chin", "imparting an indescribable hardness to the countenance, otherwise so voluptuous and buxom."

Jane comments on their welcome: "A certain superciliousness of look, coolness of manner, nonchalance of tone..." But Jane is no longer a sitting target for their superior attitudes, nor can she be hurt in the way she once was. Jane's emotional spectrum has been enlarged by falling in love; she has experienced "pains and pleasures so much more acute and exquisite" than anything she might feel as a result of the sisters' indifference, and she deals with them now in a way quite unlike her old manner: where once she used to "shrink from arrogance" - and would have quit Gateshead the next day - now she resolves to adhere to her mission to see the mother and settle things between them.

MEETING WITH MRS REED

With her newfound maturity, Jane has forgiven Mrs Reed: "It is a happy thing that time quells the longings of vengeance, and hushes the promptings of rage and aversion...I came back to her now with...a stong yearning to forget and forgive all injuries - to be reconciled and clasp hands in amity."

But Mrs Reed has *not* thawed; she looks at Jane "icily" and with a "stony eye"; it seems that "she was resolved to consider me bad to the last". Jane's old emotions return with a rush: "I felt pain, and then I felt ire; and then I felt a determination to subdue her".

Mrs Reed wants to "talk some things over" with Jane; but then she seems to lose her bearings and asks Jane who she is, referring to Jane in the third person, as if she is not there, complaining about her behaviour and even wishing her dead from the epidemic that had hit Lowood.

So as not to disquiet Mrs Reed, Jane refers to herself abstractly, while Mrs Reed explains her antipathy for Jane's mother, the sister of Mrs Reed's husband, and much beloved by him (causing immense jealousy in Mrs Reed), and how she "hated" Jane as soon as she saw her, after her husband determined to raise the baby himself when his sister died. Mrs Reed even adds that he preferred Jane to his own children; additional resentment on Mrs Reed's behalf was incurred when her husband made her swear, on *his* deathbed, to raise Jane as one of her children. Then Mrs Reed talks of her fears for her son John (she does not yet know that he has killed himself).

Ten days pass before Jane speaks to Mrs Reed again. Jane keeps busy with her imaginative drawings, as well as rendering a likeness of Rochester, whom Georgiana calls "an ugly man" when she sees it. (How important it is for Jane that Rochester is, in his own way, as unattractive facially as she thinks she is. She wants equality in every aspect of their union. Their marriage cannot take place until everything between them has, in Bronte's mind, been *equalized*.)

Eliza calls Georgiana "vain and absurd" one day, and in her tirade tells her sister that after their mother's death, "I wash my hands of you…you and I will be as separate as if we had never known each other." Georgiana responds that "Everybody knows you are the most selfish, heartless creature in existence…"

On Jane's next visit to her aunt, Mrs Reed admits that she has "twice done…a wrong" to Jane; the first time, in breaking her promise to her husband to raise Jane as one of her own, and the second she balks at revealing, but then decides she must tell Jane before it is too late. She shows Jane a letter from her uncle, John Eyre of Madeira, asking for Jane's address so that he may adopt her as his own and bequeath to her his fortune on his death. *The letter is three years old.*

On being asked why she had said nothing, Mrs Reed tells Jane that it was because she disliked her so much and that Jane's outburst against her (see Ch.4) had made her feel threatened. Jane requests her aunt's forgiveness for her unruliness (being but a child), but Mrs Reed ignores this and tells Jane she wrote to her uncle – and told him his niece was dead! And while her "last hour is racked" by the recollection of that deed, Jane was "born to torment her" and has "a very bad disposition". Jane responds that she is "passionate, but not vindictive", and that many a time she wished they could have been reconciled. And now she asks her aunt to kiss her, but, no, "she would not touch" Jane's cheek.

"Love me, then, or hate me, as you will," Jane says to her aunt; "you have my full and free forgiveness…" But Jane recognises that Mrs Reed will not change now, in spite of the lateness of the day: "living, she had ever hated me – dying, she must hate me still."

Mrs Reed dies that night. Jane feels nothing; while looking at the body, she experiences only "a sombre tearless dismay at the fearfulness of death in such a form." Eliza displays no emotion at her mother's demise, and, while Georgiana does weep, they are the tears of guilt, not love, and she will not look at her mother's corpse.

Chapter 22

Jane stays a month at Gateshead. Eliza tells her: "you perform your own part in life, and burden no one." Mrs Reed, however, would not have agreed with her daughter's opinion. Eliza reveals that she is leaving for a nunnery on the continent (and in the future she will give her portion of the family fortune, if there is anything left after brother John's extravagance, to the convent she enters). Georgiana eventually gets married to "a wealthy worn-out man of fashion".

Jane ponders what she will do after Rochester gets married to Blanche. "Where was I to go?" This question is one that Jane is obliged to ask herself at key points in the story; she asks it again when she is forced to flee Thornfield on the discovery of Bertha and the cancellation of her wedding. A home and a family are all that she has ever wanted.

Meanwhile, Jane is consumed with thoughts of seeing Rochester again, while simultaneously torturing herself with the belief that he will soon exit from her life forever: "Hasten! Be with him while you may: but a few more days or weeks, at most, and you are parted with him for ever!"

Jane thinks to herself: "I strangled a new-born agony - a deformed thing which I could not persuade myself to own and rear"; a very strange and unattractive thought, indeed, and one following many thoughts and dreams of "new-borns". The image of an infant flows through the story, as does childhood - especially an unhappy or "deformed" childhood, the like of which Jane had to endure. It is significant, perhaps, that at the end of the story, when Jane tells us that she has been married to Rochester for ten years and has had a child with him, she says nothing more of the child - of the joy that the child has brought her, of how the infant has repaired her mental scars from childhood, or of what she wishes for the child in the future. Nothing. We must make of that what we may. One final, bitter irony on the subject of children and their ghostly, metaphorical presence in Jane Eyre: when Charlotte Bronte did finally get married, she died some nine months later, and there is conjecture, if not evidence, that her death was the result of complications during pregnancy from a malady known as hyperemesis gravidurum - a condition in which the host body rejects the pregnancy. Could this fetus have become, in Charlotte Bronte's mind, the "deformed thing which I could not persuade myself to own and rear"?

RETURN TO THORNFIELD

As Jane approaches Thornfield, she finds Rochester on a stile with a book in his hand (as with her first meeting, it is held outdoors, as if there is some barrier to cross with Rochester before Jane can enter the house itself). Immediately, contrary to any expectation that he might express delight at seeing her again, given that he was so reluctant to let her go in the first place, Rochester begins teasing her for her response to his questions, calling her an "elf" and an "ignis fatuus" (will o'the wisp), and telling her she had forgotten all about him while away; the same teasing casual attitude he was wont to use on her is back, and probably because he feels hurt that she was away for so long. (His ego, while huge, is, like most egos of similar size, very fragile.) Nonetheless, Jane is filled with delight at his welcome. Her thoughts, on seeing him again, take flight – almost literally: "...there was ever in Mr Rochester (so at least I thought) such a wealth of the power of communicating happiness, that to taste but of the crumbs he scattered to stray and stranger birds like me, was to feast genially."

Rochester now turns to the subject of his (illusory) marriage to Blanche, boasting of his new carriage and how much it will suit her, and asking Jane if she has some magic potion to make him more handsome. He just will *not* relent in persisting with this painful comedy. Jane responds drily that "it would be past the power of magic". Rochester smiles at Jane, and "it was the real sunshine of feeling – he shed it over me now." Jane cannot resist thanking Rochester "for his great kindness", adding that "wherever you are is my home, – my only home." That is one *serious* admission of dependence. It gives Rochester all the certainty he needs with regard to Jane's feelings. Such a gushing, emotive statement puts her firmly in his power – a situation she has avoided at all costs until now.

The reader may well question why Jane is relaxing control over her feelings now – a tendency she has warned herself against repeatedly, with regard to Rochester – at the very moment when she is apparently about to lose him forever to Blanche. Maybe her reserve has been dissolved in desperation, now that she believes she really *will* lose him, and she is prepared to make a final appeal to him, so that he knows where she stands.

The statement Jane makes, calling Rochester "my only home", signifies how important the idea of a home is to her – safety, shelter, warmth, love – all the things she has lacked in life. Her love for Rochester *is* the home she has always sought.

Jane continues to mull over what she sees as the inevitable and imminent farewell, and she prays that "we might not be parted far or soon", and that he would "even after his marriage, keep us together somewhere under the shelter of his protection, and not quite exiled from the sunshine of his presence." Clearly she has forgotten what she said to him before – that with his marriage to Blanche settled, she would have to find a new position (far) away from him.

A fortnight passes. No further preparations for the marriage appear to be in progress. Jane begins to hope it may have been cancelled. "Never had he called me more frequently to his presence; never been kinder to me when there – and, alas! Never had I loved him so well."

In the back of her mind, somewhere in the thicket of beaten down hopes, she believes that Rochester really wants her, not Blanche.

Chapter 23

ROCHESTER FINALLY ADMITS HIS LOVE

It is now midsummer. Jane walks in the orchard early one evening. Rochester, by the scent of his cigar, announces his proximity. Jane tries to avoid him, but, of course, he knows she is there. Rochester teases Jane, insinuating that she will soon leave Thornfield, as she proposes to do when he is married, which he says he will be in about a month. He suggests a post for her in Ireland with a Mrs Dionysius O'Gall of Bitternutt Lodge (a title full of sarcastic connotations: Dionysius is the god of ecstasy, none of which Jane will have; gall=bitterness; "Bitter" and "nutt" – the meaning is clear). He is *still* making fun of her, knowing that she is suffering horribly; it seems to be an irresistible impulse in him, one that is inappropriate, to say the least, given that he knows all too well by now how she feels about him. Jane, too stricken with the thought of leaving, does not get the joke. Her reply is simple: that it is a great distance "from *you*, sir".

And then Jane begins to weep (at last her self-control gives way to her rapidly rising, finally erupting emotions). This is the first time she has cried – over a man, anyway. Her churning feelings, Rochester's teasing, his upcoming marriage, her necessary departure from Thornfield – it is too much for her. Yet Rochester continues to provoke her, claiming both that she has a hold on him – and then that she will forget him. (What is he trying to do – break her in two? Or himself?)

The pivotal moment is coming, the declaration of love on both sides. Jane tells the reader:

"The vehemence of emotion, stirred by grief and love within me, was claiming mastery, and struggling for full sway; and asserting a right to predominate: to overcome, to live, to rise, and reign at last; yes – and to speak."

The truth will out, eventually. Jane begins her oration – a last, desperate appeal to force Rochester to show his hand – in a minor key, rapidly building to a crescendo. She tells Rochester how much she will miss Thornfield: "I have lived in it a full and delightful life…I have not been trampled on. I have not been petrified. I have not been buried with inferior minds, and excluded from every glimpse of communion with what is bright and energetic, and high. I have talked, face to face, with what I reverence; with what I delight in, – with an original, a vigorous, an expanded mind. I have known you, Mr Rochester, and it strikes me with terror and anguish to feel I absolutely must be torn from you for ever. I see the necessity of departure; and it is like looking on the necessity of death."

After such a fulsome speech, such a homage to his ego, any normal male would promptly proceed to embrace her – but not Rochester, no, not he. His mind is like a No Man's Land where two opposing armies do battle (guilt and desire), and where the barbed wire of propriety and the deep trenches of remembrance mark the boundaries. He is at war with himself, and every time he makes progress towards a resolution, he is forced to retreat. But this time his reticence (or obstinacy) sparks Jane's anger as much as her affection, and she responds to him with a fierce and heartfelt lecture, the culminating monologue of her passion and frustration:

"Do you think I can stay to become nothing to you? Do you think I am an automaton?…Do you think, because I am poor, obscure, plain, and little, I am soulless and heartless? – You think wrong! – I have as much soul as you, and full as much heart! And if God had gifted me with some beauty, and much wealth, I should have made it as hard for you to leave me, as it is now for me to leave you. I am not talking to you now through the medium of custom, conventionalities, nor even of mortal flesh: – it is my spirit that addresses your spirit; just as if both had passed through the grave, and we stood at God's feet, equal, – as we are!"

We have noted several times that Jane's supreme wish is for equality (to be recognised for what she is, not for what she does not have), but that equality cannot and will not happen until the end of the story; at this point, the only equality with Rochester that Jane can imagine is posthumous.

However, Jane's powerful speech finally sounds the trumpet to Rochester's simmering but suppressed desire, and he takes Jane in his arms. Jane, whether shocked, thrilled, or overwhelmed, practically ignores the embrace and continues her rant, telling Rochester that he is marrying an inferior whom he does not truly love, that she would scorn such a union. She concludes with: "therefore I am better than you – let me go!"

To Jane's repeated avowal that she must leave him, Rochester at last reveals himself: "I offer you my hand, my heart, and a share of all my possessions." And he must repeat the offer at length before Jane accepts that this is the truth, admitting also to her that neither does he love Blanche, nor she him. "I must have you for my own – entirely my own", he says. Jane has made up his mind for him with her confession of love. Would he ever have come to the point without her explosion of feeling?

And then, at the moment when they pledge themselves each to the other, a storm commences and lightning comes crashing down. The pair hurry back to the house, where Rochester embraces her "repeatedly" – partly witnessed by Mrs Fairfax, to the latter's immense chagrin.

In the morning, it is discovered that the lightning-bolt has split "the great horse-chestnut" in two. The tree has been divided down the middle. An augury of events to come for the union between Jane and Rochester.

Chapter 24

Jane experiences a swift and sweeping transformation; now she knows she is loved by the man she loves, she acquires a whole new appearance.

"I looked at my face in the glass, and felt it was no longer plain: there was hope in its aspect, and life in its colour..."

Next day, Rochester greets her with an embrace. "It seemed natural: it seemed genial to be so well-loved, so caressed by him." (How marvellous - and ridiculous - we humans are: angry, bitter, depressed, suicidal - but once we know we are loved, we become someone else entirely.)

Rochester wants to marry Jane "in four weeks" (the sooner the better, as far as he is concerned: marry Jane, leave the country, avoid Bertha). But Jane, with her visionary mind, foreshadows the imminent discovery of Bertha when she responds to Rochester's claim that she will soon be Mrs Rochester by stating: "It can never be, sir; it does not sound likely. Human beings never enjoy complete happiness in this world. I was not born for a different destiny to the rest of my species: to imagine such a lot befalling me is a fairy tale - a day-dream..." At this point in the story, with Bertha very much alive and kicking, Jane is absolutely right: it *is* a dream - a nightmare.

Rochester blithely disagrees with her pessimism and points out the arrangements he is making for the wedding. "You are a beauty in my eyes," he tells Jane when she balks at his intention to purchase fine clothes for her. Jane strongly resists the idea of being dressed up like a happy (and wealthy) bride. Is it a lack of self-confidence, or a presentiment that all is not right?

Rochester call her "delicate and aerial" (aerial = made of air = Eyre); perhaps Jane's name also alludes to Ariel, a magical sprite from The Tempest (Rochester has frequently called her a fairy; and if Jane is Ariel, is Rochester the "earthy" man from the same play, Caliban?).

Now that Rochester has revealed his desire after so much prevarication and procrastination, he wants to make a big fuss over her. But Jane, resolute as ever, is not having any of it, as she curtly informs him:

"I love you most dearly: far too dearly to flatter you. Don't flatter me."

"I am not an angel...and I will not be one till I die: I will be myself."

(And on the subject of the fluctuations of male desire, Jane is exceedingly well-informed: "I suppose your love will effervesce in six months, or less", she tells Rochester, meaning that, like champagne, the "effervescence", or bubbling over, will fade away. Jane takes this duration of six months from her knowledge of "books written by men". For someone with so little experience of them, Jane seems to know the male sex all too well.)

Rochester insists to Jane that he will be constant: "...to the clear eye and eloquent tongue, to the soul made of fire, and the character that bends but does not break – at once supple and stable, tractable and consistent – I am ever tender and true." Fine words, very noble – they may even have been orated once to Bertha.

Rochester praises Jane; Jane disbelieves him. After one of his eulogies, she asks: "Have you ever experience of such a character, sir? Did you ever love such a one?" And he replies: "I love it now", adding, "I never met your likeness." The more relaxed and trusting Rochester feels towards Jane, the more truth he speaks.

Jane asks the question the answer to which we would all like to know: why Rochester went to such pains to make her believe he would marry Blanche. And Rochester tells her (after a moment of terror when he thought Jane might be about to ask what was *really* going on in the Thornfield attic) that he wished to make her as madly in love with him as he was with her. But was it necessary to make her so unhappy in order to arrive at the destination towards which they were both always and inevitably heading? No, Rochester has a bullying streak in him: he *likes* taunting people.

But Jane is too far gone in love to object to Rochester's character or his past behaviour at this stage, for as she so transparently states: "I loved him very much – more than I could trust myself to say – more than words had power to express." And if Jane, who gives free rein to practically every passing thought, has run out of things to say, she really *must* love him beyond words.

Jane asks Rochester to make Mrs Fairfax, who saw them embracing in the hall, aware of the true situation, which he does. Mrs Fairfax talks to Jane, confessing that she can scarcely believe that Rochester has asked her to marry him; she cannot shake the feeling that Jane is getting herself into something that might cause her pain. Jane, however, becomes "truly irritated" at Mrs Fairfax's quibbling on the matter. (Mrs Fairfax cannot know about Bertha, or she would surely have told Jane. And yet some of the other female servants seem to be aware of the situation; for example, the scene where Jane overhears two of them whispering together – which makes it very unlikely that Mrs Fairfax would not one day have heard some gossip.)

Rochester takes Jane (and Adele, at Jane's request) to choose clothes and jewels for the wedding, which inspires in Jane "annoyance and degradation"; she does not like being treated like a pet and resolves to write to her uncle John to tell him she will be married, with the idea that one day she will be the beneficiary of his estate and thus financially independent.

Jane wants to continue as the governess until they are married, with no special treatment until then. Mrs Fairfax approves her behaviour.

"Yet after all my task was not an easy one", Jane thinks to herself, "often I would rather have pleased than teased him. My future husband was becoming to me my whole world; and more than the world: almost my hope of heaven. He stood between me and every thought of religion, as an eclipse intervenes between man and the broad sun. I could not, in those days, see God for his creature: of whom I had made an idol."

For the first time in Jane's young life, God's role as her "master" is usurped by a mortal, but when Rochester falls from grace after the discovery of Bertha, she turns once more to God for succor; however, His hold over Jane never resumes its former supremacy, because Rochester never leaves her heart. At the end of the book, Jane places both God and Rochester on an even footing, giving them equal homage. In all matters, whether mundane, amorous, or devout, Jane seeks *equality*, fairness.

Chapter 25

The wedding day approaches. The trunks are packed. Jane is still unsure of becoming Mrs Rochester. Jane goes to the orchard and inspects the bifurcated tree; she notices the "firm base and strong roots" which have kept the two halves from falling apart. "You did right to hold fast to each other", she says to herself. This sequence is a metaphor for Jane's parting from Rochester, her continuing faith in him, and their eventual reunion. While noting that the tree's days of perennial growth are gone, she thinks: "You are not desolate: each of you has a comrade to sympathize with him in his decay." This proleptic (future-seeing) comment hints at Jane's and Rochester's life together after they marry.

Jane awaits Rochester's return from some mission that necessitated his being away from Thornfield for the day. Impatient to see him, she ventures out and finds him approaching on his horse. When he sees Jane, Rochester displays "some boastful triumph; which I swallowed as well as I could" - even so much in love, Jane is always aware of her position and whether she feels at ease in it. Love may make some people oblivious of anything other than the love object, but Jane is not one of these: she safeguards her private self.

Jane tells Rochester that "Everything in life seems unreal." After dinner they sit together. Jane is gripped by some strong feeling, a sense of impending change: "who knows with what fate the next [hour] may come charged?" she says to Rochester. Somehow, she knows that everything is not quite in place for her future happiness. Jane tells Rochester what is on her mind. It is the suspicion of an obstacle - "a strange regretful consciousness of some barrier dividing us" is how she describes it. The barrier - and *what* a barrier - is Bertha.

Jane tells Rochester of her recent dream: she was walking on a road in charge of "a little child", crying and shivering, while Rochester pulled ahead in the distance. Rochester tells her to forget her "visionary woe", but that is Jane's gift, her imagination. In the dream, she sees Rochester disappearing, and her love for him, perhaps, is the child. Then she tells Rochester of another dream: Thornfield is ruined, abandoned, "the retreat of bats and owls"; she still carries the child; Rochester rides away on his horse "departing for many years, and for a distant country." The dream ends with Jane letting go of the child, falling, and waking. Our dreams usually tell us more about ourselves than about the future, but in this case...

BERTHA'S INCURSION INTO JANE'S ROOM

Now the nightmare becomes a reality. The night before the wedding, Jane awakens to see Bertha in the room, putting on her veil. Jane tells Rochester it looked like a vampire. Then the creature tears her veil in two (echo of the split tree trunk) and tramples on it. The figure approaches Jane's bed - "the fiery eye glared at me" - and Jane passes out from terror. (Perhaps we should ask why Bertha didn't just strangle Jane there and then - she was prepared to gash her own brother, why not Jane, the bride-to-be of her hated-to-hell husband, Rochester?) Jane later describes "a savage face", "red eyes", and "blackened inflation of the lineaments". To which Rochester tartly replies: "Ghosts are usually pale, Jane." (Pretty cool response from someone who is about to marry bigamously and hasn't told his new bride about the old one.)

Jane spends the night in Adele's room. The next morning, without having slept, she prepares herself "to meet, the dread, but adored, type of my unknown future day."

When Jane asks Rochester to tell her who it was in her room, he says, "The creature of an over-stimulated brain", refusing to offer any more satisfactory answer; he will not allow that it happened, calling it a dream, and telling Jane that Thornfield is obviously not demolished, and he is still by her side. "Am I severed from you by insuperable obstacles? Am I leaving you without a tear - without a kiss - without a word?" Rochester asks. Jane responds: "Not yet."

Again, Jane knows something (their imminent separation) that Rochester will not even envisage as a possibility; he has simply refused to imagine any thought of an obstacle to his future satisfaction. Then he tries to explain away the visitation in Jane's room by claiming that it must have been Grace Poole. And he will say no more. Such behaviour indicates a man who has yet to repent and reform (as Jane suggested he should do) - a man who has still not learned to take responsibility for his actions.

Chapter 26

THE WEDDING - ANNULLED

Jane dresses for the wedding. Rochester is impatient and distracted (we know why). There are no guests. "I wanted to feel the thoughts whose force he seemed breasting and resisting," Jane thinks to herself as Rochester hastens to complete the act. Jane espies two strangers hovering in the vicinity of the church; somehow she knows they will enter. Once inside, "two shadows only moved in a remote corner." When Mr Wood the clergyman asks the portentous question – whether there is any obstacle to the marriage – someone steps forward to affirm that there is. Rochester ignores the claimant and demands continuance; Mr Wood will not accede. The newcomer asserts that there is "an insuperable impediment" to the union.

One of the visitors now utters the dreadful words: "Mr Rochester has a wife now living." Jane reveals that "My nerves vibrated to those low-spoken words as they had never vibrated to thunder – my blood felt their subtle violence as it had never felt frost or fire..." Rochester's "whole face was colourless rock: his eye was both spark and flint." He stiffens, grasps Jane. The man who spoke is Briggs, a solicitor; he produces a statement from Richard Mason, the brother, attesting to the previous marriage. Now Mason himself, the second of the shadows, steps forward. He asserts that Bertha is at Thornfield Hall.

Rochester is silent "for ten minutes" then announces that the marriage is off. "Bigamy is an ugly word! – I meant, however, to be a bigamist: but fate has outmanoeuvred me...Gentlemen, my plan is broken up!" he says blithely – with Jane standing in a state of numbed shock right beside him. Then he relates the sorry tale of Bertha and invites everyone to go with him to witness her existence.

Inside the hidden room, at last revealed, Grace is tending her. Bertha leaps at Rochester like a cornered animal. With help, she is restrained. Rochester pleads with the assembly, tries to explain his predicament.

Briggs tells Jane that she is cleared of all blame and reveals that Mason, through his business dealings, knows her uncle in Madeira, which is how the solicitor heard of Jane's impending marriage to Rochester, through the letter Jane sent her uncle. Jane's uncle has been taken ill and is confined to bed.

The group disperses and Jane locks herself into her room. She reviews the day's events: "...nothing had smitten me, or scathed me, or maimed me. And yet, where was the Jane Eyre of yesterday? - where was her life? - where were her prospects?"

What Jane fears most has come to pass: she has failed to break free of the limits of her small life. She is back where she started. "Jane Eyre, who had been an ardent, expectant woman - almost a bride - was a cold, solitary girl again: her life was pale; her prospects were desolate."

Jane can no longer view Rochester in the incandescent light of her former intense love. She sees all too well now, and her only recourse is to leave. "Oh, how blind had been my eyes! How weak my conduct!" Jane reverts to her old habit of vehement self-criticism. She puts the blame for the debacle on herself, not Rochester. Her only comfort now - as it always had been before Rochester - is God.

Chapter 27

Jane resolves that she must leave Thornfield "at once". She wavers at the thought of the gargantuan effort necessary to tear herself away from Rochester. She stumbles out of her room at last; Rochester has been waiting for her. He tries to explain himself while still retaining his pride; he asks for forgiveness. Jane inwardly gives it, but will not speak. She is too weakened from shock, too perplexed to condemn him. She imagines she would like to die at that moment, because "I must leave him, it appears. I do not want to leave him - I cannot leave him."

Rochester now tries to manipulate her into feeling guilty for rejecting him (he owes Jane an apology, and much more, but he wants her to surrender to him before he issues it). He praises her, trumpets his love for her - but he wants her to go and live with him "in solitude" (i.e., unmarried, and far away from nosy people). He almost becomes violent when Jane rejects his offer. "But I was not afraid: not in the least", Jane thinks, "I felt an inward power; a sense of influence, which supported me." Jane has her principles, and one of the strongest is not to permit other people to take advantage of her. Rochester, however, has only one principle: domination. But Jane is his match in the battle of wills.

Her strength almost extinguished, Jane breaks down and begins to weep. Rochester, pressing his advantage, accuses her of never loving him – or, if she did, only for his status. (His behaviour really is insupportable.) Jane tells him that she will leave. At this, Rochester announces in desperation: "I am not married." He becomes even more agitated. He warns her that he is losing control. He tries to make her touch him; then he tries to touch her. He craves physical contact with her just as he knows that she is pulling away.

Rochester changes tack, seeking to overcome her resistance with the story of his "sad" life: how his father, "an avaricious, rasping man" left everything to Rochester's older brother, Rowland (that was customary in the 1800s); how Rochester was sent to Jamaica to marry the daughter of a former business acquaintance of his father, a Mr Mason, in order to secure her fortune; Rochester relates how he was "dazzled, stimulated" by her, how he was encouraged by her relatives, yet "I never loved, I never esteemed, I did not even know her". Then the reader has to ask: Why? Why did he go along with it? Who was forcing him? No one, it seems: Rochester was overcome with desire for this exotic Caribbean woman, and he was too headstrong and immature to consider the consequences.

After the marriage, Rochester learned that the bride's mother was "only mad" and consigned to an asylum. Rochester claims his father and brother knew this but kept silent in order to obtain the £30,000 fortune that was coming to Bertha; what benefit it would bring to *them* is unclear. Her family concealed Bertha's true age, which was five years older than Rochester's, and Rochester soon found that his wife was uncongenial: she had a nature "wholly alien", and "tastes obnoxious" to him. She could not converse intelligently (presumably they did not converse much before the marriage – Rochester just leapt on her), yet he tried to repress his "repentance and disgust" and "deep antipathy". For the money? For the sake of propriety? We are given no explanation.

Rochester lived with Bertha for four years. She turned into a monster "intemperate and unchaste". (How could she be "unchaste" if she was married to Rochester? And if she was being unchaste outside the marriage, he could have divorced her, surely. This sounds like a classic tale of male depravity: what fascinated him sexually at the beginning of the affair turned to disgust when he had sated himself.) Then Rochester's brother died, and Rochester was chained to "a nature the most gross, impure, depraved" he had ever been exposed to, apparently. Bertha became nightmarish in her drama and spectacle (what we would call "acting out" nowadays). He was now 26. Jane tells Rochester that she pities him. He claims that he considered suicide, but decided to return to Europe, confine his wife at Thornfield, have her cared for, and then travel. (That's one way of dealing with the problem - imprison your legal wife in a dingy room while you go off whoring in Europe.)

There appears, at least to this reader, to be a lot of disingenuous self-justification in the way Rochester convinced himself that what he was doing was acceptable - not just to the world, but to himself. As he relates it to Jane, he justified his course of action thus: "You may take the maniac with you to England; confine her with due attendance and precautions at Thornfield; then travel yourself to what clime you will, and form what new tie you like. That woman, who has so abused your long-suffering - so sullied your name; so outraged your honour; so blighted your youth - is not your wife; nor are you her husband. See that she is cared for as her condition demands, and you have done all that God and Humanity require of you. Let her identity, her connection with yourself, be buried in oblivion: you are bound to impart them to no living being. Place her in safety and comfort: shelter her degradation with secrecy, and leave her."

Did Rochester *really* do enough to acquit himself with honour? Why didn't he call on the medical profession to care for her - even to cure her, if possible? Was it because he did not *want* her to recover, which would mean resuming his duties, in name if nothing else, as husband? There is a case for claiming that he did *not* desire her recovery at all; in that way he could continue to play the victim and go about his life without guilt – and without Bertha round his neck. But his behaviour is not to his credit. Rochester is not quite as human or humane as he would want the world (or himself) to think, and that, in turn, begs the question of what turned Bertha mad: her genealogy (madness in the family) – or his acute disdain for her?

Rochester senior, who had no desire to make public the marriage when his son told him his feelings about Bertha, kept the secret. So Rochester went back to England and locked her in the attic at Thornfield, where she has now been for ten years. Ten years in a room! Grace Poole and the surgeon Carter were the only two who knew the truth. "The lunatic is both cunning and malignant", Rochester claims, and has on several occasions outwitted Grace (as we well know). But who wouldn't become cunning – or malignant – locked up for a decade? And yet, even though Bertha could, and did, find a way out of her room, *she never tried to escape from Thornfield*. Was that because she still loved Rochester, in spite of what he had done to her?

Jane asks Rochester how he could have even considered another marriage while Bertha was still alive, to which he replies: "I had determined, and was convinced that I could and ought." In other words, having locked her up, he felt free to carry on *as if she did not exist*. The response of someone who has repressed all personal guilt in the matter. Perhaps Rochester *had* suffered; let us say that he definitely *did* – but what about *Bertha's* suffering? That did not seem to matter to him.

So Rochester travelled throughout Europe, looking for "my ideal of a woman"; none satisfied (how could they, when his hostility to Bertha had turned him not just against her – but against *every* woman?). "I tried dissipation – never debauchery: that I hated, and hate," he says. The difference between dissipation and debauchery is so subtle as to be undiscernible – Rochester probably means by dissipation that he only had one woman at a time, and that debauchery might have meant orgies. But the frame of mind is pretty much the same for both: the man is trying to blot out his unpleasant and unhappy thoughts through saturation of the senses. Neither dissipation nor debauchery is a cure for that; the thoughts will not go away just because they are smothered.

His first attachment was Celine Varens, but that did not come off; then others. "You think me an unfeeling, loose-principled rake: don't you?" he asks Jane, who is still so in love that she can only weakly respond, "I don't like you so well as I have done, sometimes...". Rochester *wants* to bring blame and disgust down on himself; it is plain to see that he is consumed with self-loathing as a result of his actions - locking up Bertha, trying to forget about her, and going off to Europe on a sexual spree. The problem, of course, was not dealt with; indeed, no, the problem continued to worsen. Bertha became wilder and more like an animal as a result of being treated like one. Ten years in the same room.

Rochester admits that his rakish lifestyle now appals him: "to live familiarly with inferiors is degrading. I now hate the recollection of the time..." But the ease with which he casts the women he enjoyed as *inferiors* does not do him much credit - and, strangely, having erred with his selection of Bertha as his wife, having paid for that error as she turned against him, and having locked her up to contain her indiscretions (and his), you might think he would go in the other direction and look for a type the opposite of his wife; but his own nature drives him further *down* into the pit, not *up* into the skies. Until Jane arrives on the scene.

Jane, naturally enough, is cautious, hearing Rochester's story: "I drew...the certain inference, that if I were so far to forget myself...to become the successor of these poor girls, he would one day regard me with the same feeling which now in his mind desecrated their memory." Exactly. Jane has recognised that Rochester is - if not innately, then as a result of his experiences with Bertha and the women thereafter - a misogynist.

Rochester continues his story (seeing clearly the disapproval on Jane's face as to his earlier disclosures): at a low point in his life, despondent after all the disappointments (of his own making, to be sure), he stumbles upon Jane (literally, while on his horse), who from the first moment strikes him as someone not simply out for herself. But how does he treat Jane initially? Like a toy, a pet, or some other new diversion. He *played* with her, as he surely played with the other women who came before. As he himself says: "I liked what I had seen, and wished to see more...Yet, for a long time, I treated you distantly...I was an intellectual epicure, and wished to prolong the gratification of making this novel and piquant acquaintance..." Indeed! "Prolonging the gratification" is a phrase straight out of the debauchee's handbook. Gratification - the stirring of the senses, the slaking of the appetite - is everything to such a person. It is clear to *this* reader that Rochester's probable goal with Jane - at first, anyway - was simply to *seduce* her.

But Jane is different. She does not simper, she is not coy, she does not flirt and flatter him, she speaks plainly and forthrightly when he asks his leading questions. And her behaviour, as is the way with a strong and virtuous woman, changes *him*, instead of the reverse. In a word, he is *weaker* than she is. But, and here's the rub, Jane falls in love with him, for all his faults.

When Rochester observed that Jane was softening and responding to him, he shed the ironic armour with which he had surrounded himself and started to respond to her in a real way, to the point where "I had much ado often to avoid straining you then and there to my heart." But all this verbiage comes too late to remedy the outrage and misery he has brought upon Jane, and his confessions serve only to amplify her suffering and harden her resolve: "I knew what I must do - and do soon..."

Rochester, sensing her complete withdrawal, in spite of his efforts to pacify and retain her, increases his blandishments: "I have found for the first time what I can truly love - I have found *you*...I am bound to you with a strong attachment...a solemn passion is conceived in my heart..." Rochester regards himself as a new man, bathed in Jane's adoration, and wants to "love faithfully and well" - although that depends, he says, on being "faithfully and well loved in return"; i.e., she should forget his past indiscretions and look only to the future man. Sensing that Jane is still pulling away from him, Rochester requests her utter commitment to him, her "pledge of fidelity".

"Jane, you understand what I want of you? Just this promise - 'I will be yours, Mr Rochester.'" But Jane is not the kind of person to be compromised, and the existence of Bertha is too great an obstacle for her to surmount. Rochester begins to understand that she really *is* going away. He tries to embrace her.

"This - this is wicked", Jane says.
"It would not be wicked to love me", Rochester replies.
"It would to obey you", Jane retorts.

Rochester tries again to elicit her sympathy, but now, completely detached, she will only give him this advice: "Do as I do: trust in God and yourself. Believe in heaven. Hope to meet again there." Jane has set personal relations entirely to one side now and is using God as a lever to prise herself from the man she loves but can no longer respect. It is as if she has stopped up any further feeling. She remains adamant about leaving Thornfield. Rochester panics; his voice rising, he asks petulantly:

"Then you condemn me to live wretched, and to die accursed?" Jane's answer: "I advise you to live sinless; and I wish you to die tranquil." And she follows this stark advice with: "We were born to strive and endure - you as well as I: do so. You will forget me before I forget you."

(That last sentence must have been like a hammer blow to Rochester, because it could only have been uttered with the knowledge Jane now has about his woman-hunting in Europe and his abandonment of Bertha at Thornfield. Rochester is not the person Jane thought he was, in spite of her love for him.)

And he, now losing all composure as he sees Jane slipping away from him, tries every base method to break down her defences: "You make me a liar by such language: you sully my honour...Is it better to drive a fellow-creature to despair than to transgress a mere human law...?" Rochester conveniently ignores the "despair" to which he must have driven Bertha in order for her to have become the bestial creature she now is.

Jane is moved and almost swayed by Rochester's display of deep feeling, but she does not succumb, either to his pleas or his veiled threats. She says: "I will keep the law given by God; sanctioned by man. ...Laws and principles are not for the times when there is no temptation: they are for moments such as this...stringent are they; inviolate they shall be."

Rochester, unable to convince her with words, becomes physical (an arrogant man's last resort when he is not being heard): "...he crossed the floor and seized my arm...his grip was painful..." But as soon as he has taken hold of Jane, he releases her: "If I tear, if I rend the slight prison, my outrage will only let the captive loose." He is not so insensitive or foolhardy that he does not recognise that to use physical force on Jane's frail *body* would only cause her much stronger *mind* to escape him – and with it, whatever remains of her former love. What he wants from her is her "will and energy...virtue and purity", not her "brittle frame". She would flee from him mentally, if she could not physically, in an instant. Rochester tries to embrace her a last time, but she evades him and leaves the room.

That night, Jane dreams of the red-room. This is the transitional space, the portal from an impossible situation to an uncertain future. Jane must step through and onto the other side; she must take her chances with the unknown.

Then Jane dreams of a female figue, "a white human form", which "whispered in my heart". The figure says: "My daughter, flee temptation!" Jane answers: "Mother, I will." Who is this mother? The ghost of Jane's, or the Virgin Mary, or all mothers in one?

Jane rises from her bed early and leaves Thornfield undetected, taking with her a few scraps of food in a bag – and her memories: "Mr Rochester, I will love you and live with you through life till death" is what she wants to say to him, but she will not jeopardise her resolve to leave. She will not speak to him again.

Walking in the opposite direction of Millcote, she imagines Rochester waiting for her still. "I had injured – wounded – left my master. I was hateful in my own eyes. Still I could not turn, nor retrace one step. God must have led me on."

Jane faints, rises, continues. A coach approaches; she hands over what money she has and takes a seat to any place far away. The discovery that Rochester is married, the cancellation of the wedding, the termination of all her hopes for the future have brought on a kind of breakdown. Jane has no idea where she is going, nor what she will do when she gets there. As she addresses the reader, the single thought uppermost in her mind is that she has disappointed Rochester:

"...for never may you, like me, dread to be the instrument of evil to what you wholly love."

But surely it is Rochester who is "the instrument of evil", deceiving, betraying, and then attempting to hold on to Jane in spite of everything he has done. And yet, such is the depth of her love, it is Jane who feels she has wronged *him*.

VOL.III

STAGE FIVE: THE RIVERS FAMILY

Chapter 28

The coach arrives at a place called Whitcross and Jane alights, leaving her parcel behind in error: "...and now, I am absolutely destitute." She has been dropped off at a crossroads where four roads meet. The significance of Jane finding herself at a crossroads at this stage of the story is worth noting: Bronte was clearly making and marking an important "junction".

- A crossroads represents both choice and uncertainty: which direction will Jane take? Will she have the courage to go into the unknown, or will she go back to perceived safety (Rochester)?
- A crossroads represents both a crisis and an opportunity: does Jane have the mental strength to pass through the first to reach the second?
- A "four-road" crossroads can also represent the four points of the compass; there is a random choice to be made, and Jane is throwing herself on the mercy of providence.

Surrounded on all sides by the open countryside – moorlands, fields of heather, mountains (a daunting vista when you have nowhere to shelter and no food) – Jane calls on Mother Nature to protect her: "Not a tie holds me to human society at this moment…I have no relative but the universal mother, nature…" And she adds to that, somewhat hopefully: "Nature…benign and good; I thought she loved me, outcast as I was…"

The beauty of the landscape is no comfort to Jane, however; now that she is alone in the emptiness, she apprehends the enormity of her break with Rochester, who gave her a home and a future (even if unacceptable on the terms offered). She asks herself once more the questions that have been haunting her all her life:

"What was I to do? Where to go?"

Jane finds herself in a new, hostile, indeed overwhelming situation; and – like her experiences with the Reeds, Lowood School, and now at the hands of Rochester – not of her own making, but thrust on her by circumstances beyond her control. Yes, in Rochester's case, Jane did have a choice – but it was between becoming his mistress or retaining her integrity. There was no choice for someone like Jane, really.

Jane forages for berries, tries to sleep, but her thoughts as always return to Rochester. Her "sad heart…bemoaned him with bitter pity…demanded him with ceaseless longing…"

The environment in which Jane finds herself, and her reaction to it, seems to suggest a deliberate reference by Bronte to the Romantic movement (c. 1790-1830), characterized by the artist's wonder at God's awe-inspiring creations in the natural world, measured against man's (and woman's) relative insignificance.

"God is everywhere", Jane proclaims, "but certainly we feel His presence most when His works are on the grandest scale spread before us: and it is in the unclouded night-sky, where His worlds wheel their silent course, that we read clearest His infinitude, His omnipotence."

Then she prays for Rochester, hoping that "Mr Rochester was safe: he was God's and by God would he be guarded." (And yet he must suffer blindness and the loss of a limb before God is satisfied that he has paid for his sins. Jane never comments on this divine justice, or lack of it, concerning Rochester's injuries; Rochester, however, believes that he has been justly treated by God, because judgement has been tempered with mercy.)

Jane beds down on the heather, but the next day is hot, and the precariousness of her situation begins to dawn on her. She has no money, no food, no one from whom to seek help. She even has a fleeting wish to have died in the night, "absolved by death from further conflict with fate…"

However, she is a true Christian, and the longing for death is soon dismissed, because "Life, however, was yet in my possession; with all its requirements, and pains, and responsibilities. The burden must be carried; the want provided for; the suffering endured; the responsibility fulfilled." Jane will not allow herself to succumb to despair.

She draws near to a village. "I must struggle on: strive to live and bend to toil like the rest." She looks for help, for sustenance, amongst the inhabitants, and receives very little charity, managing only to extract some bits of food from unwilling givers. Where is the Christian goodwill, the generosity? As already discussed, Bronte uses *Jane Eyre* to argue out and debate the principles of the Christian faith (evangelicalism, hypocrisy, the afterlife, etc.) as they are applied by ordinary people, but what is she saying here, one wonders? From these scenes of Jane being turned away, first in this village, and then by the servant at Moor House, we might well conclude that Bronte does *not* believe that there is *any* Christian charity amongst common folk.

"Shall I be an outcast again this night?" Jane asks herself. "…who will receive me?…this total prostration of hope…why cannot I reconcile myself to the prospect of death? Why do I struggle to retain a valueless life? Because I know or believe Mr Rochester is still living…"

In spite of all the hurt and harm he has heaped on Jane's head, she is still faithful to him; she still believes in him.

JANE FINDS THE RIVERS FAMILY

Jane leaves the village, where there is no comfort or shelter for her, and again enters the wilderness of the moors. Exhausted, desperate, she comes upon a house; she sees "Two young, graceful women...all delicacy and cultivation" with "faces full of distinction and intelligence." As Jane looks in through the window, she listens and learns that they are reading in German (her kind of educated folk), and that their father recently passed on.

Jane knocks. Hannah the servant answers, mistrustfully. (Here Bronte uses dialect when Hannah speaks, and it is cumbersome, a misstep to a modern reader, but Bronte was probably hoping to engage the attention of provincial readers - which she did, because *Jane Eyre* was very popular in the North of England.) Hannah tries to dismiss Jane, but she is rescued by the arrival of the brother, St John, who takes her into the house. Jane calls herself "Jane Elliott".

Once Jane is indoors, she is able to "resume" her "natural manner and character", as if she were acting a role in a drama (the outcast, the indigent) and reinhabit her real character (the artist, the intellectual). After some discussion, the Rivers receive Jane into the house as a guest, and she goes to bed "with a glow of grateful joy - and slept."

Jane has somehow survived the ordeal.

Chapter 29

Jane is in bed for three days. The Rivers inspect her from time to time, noting "a peculiar face", "an unusual physiognomy", and calling her "not at all handsome". St John Rivers offers up a particularly snide comment: "the grace and harmony of beauty are quite wanting", he says, which is ironic given that he later asks her to be his wife, even if in name only. Once again, we return to the emphasis on Jane's looks, or lack of them; it was unnecessary from the point of view of the story for the Rivers to offer up this kind of commentary, but the explanation, which follows previous similar incidents, is that Jane is again feeling vulnerable, and that is when the thoughts return (it really does not matter to Bronte who voices these insults, only that they happen in the same circumstances every time - Jane's difficulties). It is intriguing to wonder what was going on in Bronte's head when she wrote these passages; we shall never know, but it is my belief that the author often felt like this - inferior, unattractive, worthless - about *herself*. (And there is a connection between these thoughts - there always is in these cases -and Jane's eating disorder, which we discussed before).

Inside the house, there is friction at first between Hannah the servant and Jane. Jane answers her back sharply and takes some time to forgive the old woman for trying to turn her away that first night. Eventually they come to terms with each other.

The Rivers family is long settled in the area of Marsh End, Jane learns, and there is a local businessman, Mr Oliver, who owns a much bigger house than the Rivers' Moor House - a "grand hall" in Morton Vale. The Rivers children are all great readers (shades of the Bronte children), but as the family is no longer wealthy, the girls must find posts as governesses (apparently the only source of employment for educated young women at that time). Jane is free with her praise for Diana and Mary, especially the former, because Diana is the stronger character and therefore more appealing to Jane (who also has an "active will").

Jane observes St John closely for the first time, admiring his "Greek face, very pure in outline". However, she also notes "elements within either restless, or hard, or eager." He has "blue, pictorial-looking eyes", seeming "to use them rather as instruments to search other people's thoughts, than as agents to reveal his own..." It is all the more notable that St John, a man as cold as a poker but without its occasional warmth, eventually opens up almost completely to Jane; when Rochester told Jane that something in her personality invited people to speak confidingly to her, he was dead right. To St John's "unceremonious directness" of language, Jane gives as good as she gets, answering him back in similar fashion. "It is my way - it always was my way, by instinct - ever to meet the brief with brevity, the direct with plainness."

Jane gives out only limited information to the Rivers' enquiries, telling them that she was an orphan, the daughter of a clergyman, and that her parents died before she knew them; she speaks of Lowood, of Thornfield – without mentioning Rochester – and of how she was obliged to quit in a hurry, leaving everything she had behind. She admits that she is "near nineteen" and unmarried. She thanks the Rivers for their "noble hospitality", for rescuing her "from death", and especially St John for his "evangelical charity" (charity which was *not* shown by the locals earlier). She continues to call herself Jane Elliott, while admitting that it is not her real name. Jane insists that she wants to work, to be "independent". St John says he will seek out employment for her, but "if you are inclined to despise the day of small things, seek some more efficient succour than such as I can offer." Like his master, the Lord God, St John tends to give with one hand and take away with the other. His abruptness obliges Diana to apologise on his behalf to Jane, calling him "crusty" as she does so.

Chapter 30

Jane grows ever closer to Diana and Mary, enjoying "the pleasure arising from perfect congeniality of tastes, sentiments, and principles….what they approved, I reverenced." Jane reads their books and discusses them with the sisters. "Thought fitted thought; opinion met opinion; we coincided, in short, perfectly." (Diana and Mary Rivers, meet Emily and Anne Bronte.)

Diana, whom Jane calls the "leader", tutors Jane, and in return Jane shares her drawing skills. For St John, she does not feel such intimacy: "he seemed of a reserved, an abstracted, and even of a brooding nature." In spite of his devotion to charitable works, he "did not appear to enjoy that mental serenity, that inward content, which should be the reward of every sincere Christian and practical philanthropist." Indeed, "Nature was not to him that treasury of light it was to his sisters." He is, however, a powerful preacher, although Jane wonders whether "the eloquence…had sprung from a depth where lay turbid dregs of disappointment…troubling impulses of insatiate yearnings and disquieting aspirations." (Jane demonstrates a startling ability to see beneath the surface of someone's verbal camouflage.) Jane believes that St John "had not yet found that peace of God which passeth all understanding: he had no more found it, I thought, than had I; with my concealed and racking regrets for my broken idol and lost elysium...which possessed me and tyrannized over me ruthlessly." Bronte is likening Jane's longing for Rochester to something inside St John that is unsettled, and which Jane, with her acute perceptiveness, has noticed; indeed, the problem is that St John is in love with Rosamond Oliver, but because he is proud – arrogant – he considers her (in spite of her beauty, or perhaps because of it) his inferior, and he will not get involved with her, even though she has made it plain that she likes him. He is determined to remain "pure" and love only God – in notable contrast to Jane, who relinquishes her sole and solitary devotion to God in order to attach herself to Rochester. This is another reason why Jane Eyre is a very modern heroine – she leaves God for a man. That was pretty rebellious in the 1800s; at least, to admit to it in a book was.

A month goes by. Diana and Mary are due to return to their posts as governesses. St John talks zealotry to Jane. He calls himself "poor and obscure". He is even a bit snide (again) to her: "I see now your habits have been what the world calls refined"; does he also look down upon his sisters, who have similar inclinations? He employs a technique not unlike Rochester's – first taunting Jane for her perceived failings, then asking for her help when he feels he has her in his power, and she will be more likely to agree. Indeed, St John now offers Jane the role of teacher at the parish school (funded by the church); he emphasises "how poor the proposal is, – how trivial – how cramping." He is trying to put her off to confirm his worst opinion of her, while simultaneously testing her to see if she is worthy.

St John reveals that he will not stay long at Morton, now his father is dead. He delivers a confused and confusing speech to Jane, both criticising and sympathising with her, which tells us more about his own inner turmoil than it does about any weakness in Jane's character – for what is really going on inside St John's heart and soul is the battle between "propensities and principles" – between what he wants (propensities) and what he feels he *ought* to want (principles). It is – beneath the artificial, rigidly maintained surface of calm and severity he displays – the battle between complexity and simplicity, between his ambivalent sexual desire (for Rosamond) and his single-minded devotion to God. Diana tells Jane that he is preparing to leave for a long time - "it might be a parting for life."

Then news arrives that their uncle John is dead. (He is also Jane's uncle, as we later discover - she is their cousin). Diana reveals that they did not know him, that he quarrelled with their father, and, after the break, made a lot of money: "twenty thousand pounds". With his death, the Rivers each inherit a small sum, while the larger balance goes to the one other relative (Jane, although we do not know this yet). Diana bemoans the small bequest and wishes they had been given a little more.

The next day, the sisters leave for their posts, Jane departs for her new role as teacher, Mr Rivers and Hannah return to the parsonage, and Moor House is closed up.

Chapter 31

Jane recognises the potential of some of her pupils at the school (although she does refer to them on one occasion as "coarsely-clad little peasants"!). She is somewhat pessimistic about her own future, however: "Much enjoyment I do not expect in the life opening before me…", but decides she can cope with the disappointment, "if I regulate my mind, and exert my powers as I ought…" Another example of the kind of advice (*control yourself!*) that young women were expected to follow in the 19th century (as taught in self-help books of the era and invoked by sermon-spouters from church pulpits).

Nonetheless, Jane's new role is a difficult adjustment; she is all too aware that she is wasting her intelligence on such basic mentoring as teaching children to read and write, but she acknowledges these troublesome feelings, buckles down, and hopes to turn "disgust" into "gratification".

Meanwhile, her thoughts turn frequently to Rochester; Jane debates with herself whether it would have been better to compromise instead of running away, but her conclusion is that "he would have loved me well for a while" – and (what is unsaid) would have grown tired of her, as he did with the other women. However, she still believes that "he did love me – no one will ever love me so again...He was fond and proud of me – it is what no man besides will ever be." Why she is so willing to convince herself that no man other than Rochester could love her is tied into her poor opinion of her looks – she ignores, or refuses to allow, that Rochester fell in love with her *mind* first. Again, her thoughts turn back to him, and she asks herself whether it is better "to be a slave in a fool's paradise" or to be "a village-schoolmistress", and she concludes: "I feel now I was right when I adhered to principle and law, and scorned and crushed the insane promptings of a frenzied moment. God directed me to a correct choice: I thank his providence for the guidance!" (Or, I am *so* glad that I did not let myself go – I would have regretted it later.)

Jane wallows in her misery, however, mourning "for the doom which had reft me from adhesion to my master: for him I was no more to see", and she is also concerned that because she has left him, he will suffer from "desperate grief and fatal fury" that will send him back to the dark place he was in before he met her, far from "the path of right", with no hope of "ultimate restoration". His soul, she frets, will be lost forever, if (or when) he reverts to the corrupt ways of his previous life.

St John appears at her cottage; again, Jane reassures him that she is content with her accommodation and her post. "But you feel solitude an oppression?" he asks. (He has begun testing her to see if she will have the strength to be his missionary wife.) He tells Jane not to look back, but to nourish the mind with God "as strong as the forbidden food it longed to taste..." (He believes that Jane must have run away from a man, although he does not yet know the name Rochester). However, the warning about *forbidden food* is more appropriate to *his own* desires than Jane's – he is in love with Rosamond Oliver and must correct and control himself with prayer and principle every day so that he does not make a move on her, which is what he is very afraid he might soon do.

Like Rochester, St John finds himself divulging personal information to Jane, revealing that he was "miserable" a year earlier, that he longed for a more exciting career than parish priest, and that his life was "wretched" – so wretched, indeed, that he felt he had to change things or die. Then he discovered that God "had an errand" for him as a missionary, and by dedicating himself single-mindedly to this goal, he has found peace.

Now Rosamond Oliver – the source of St John's inner turmoil – arrives at the house. She teases St John, who flounders under her spell. Jane gives the reader a point-by-point description of Rosamond's feminine qualities – everything which Jane believes she lacks herself. Rosamond has "perfect beauty", complete charm, and no defects whatsoever – so Jane tells herself, delighting in Rosamond's loveliness. "I admire her with my whole heart", she thinks. Jane inevitably loses sight of her own immense qualities when comparing herself with someone superficially more attractive.

Rosamond tries to draw St John out more ("why are you so very shy, and so very sombre?"), but he steels himself against her advances. Jane realises that he is highly attracted to Rosamond, and she witnesses his "suffering and sacrifice" as he refuses to allow himself to indulge in romantic inclinations. His rigid self-control inspires Jane to master her own unhappiness over Rochester.

Chapter 32

Jane continues with her work at the school. She sees progress amongst some of her pupils (drawing from her own experience of being overlooked by adults, she devotes herself doubly to the children).

Her dreams are populated with Rochester ("again and again"), and with these reappearances Jane repeatedly experiences the loss of her "hope of passing a lifetime at his side". She always wakes in a fraught state.

Rosamond Oliver visits the school while St John is there, causing him acute embarrassment, although he works hard to stifle the signs of discomfort. Jane regards his refusal to give in to his true feelings as a result of his unswerving fealty to God and to the numerous contrary demands of his personality ("the rover, the aspirant, the poet, the priest") which could never be satisfied "in the limits of a single passion" – yet Jane ignores that this is exactly what St John is asking from God: a single passion. Jane does not underestimate Miss Oliver, however, and believes Rosamond has "an amiable caprice", but the young woman does not have a "profound mind". (Rather like Blanche Ingram, Rosamond is lovely, but no intellectual – that is Jane's advantage, her mind, although she never brags about it openly.) Rosamond asks Jane to sketch her portrait.

Rosamond's father, Mr Oliver, invites Jane to Vale Hall, his mansion. He approves of what she has done at Morton school. He reveals that long ago the Rivers family had owned "all Morton", and considers St John's desire to be a missionary as "throwing a valuable life away." Jane thinks Mr Oliver would be pleased if St John married Rosamond.

St John visits Jane and inspects her finished drawing of Rosamond. He will not admit to Jane that he even recognises the likeness (so fearful is he of showing any interest in Rosamond and thereby reawakening his desire). Jane ignores his defensiveness and begins to probe him as to his true feelings. He finally admits he loves Rosamond "so wildly", in the next instant declaring that she would be no good for him. Jane suggests he abandon his plan to become a missionary, which he rejects absolutely. Jane continues to draw him out, to the extent that "He had not imagined that a woman would dare to speak so to a man", but Jane feels "at home in this sort of discourse." St John admits that she is "original...and not timid", but he reasserts that he is "a cold, hard man" and will rebuff all emotion for Rosamond. "Reason, and not Feeling, is my guide", he states; he expatiates on what Christianity means to him, how it has brought out the best in him. But is his religious zeal *honest*, or just a defence he uses to mask his vulnerabilities: his fear of losing control, of being free to choose – of daring to love someone? He also tells Jane that he considers her "a specimen of a diligent, orderly, energetic woman", and there is something unpleasantly condescending in this description, because Jane is so much more than that. This patronising approach is, surely, part of St John's plan to dominate and subdue her so that he can compel her to go to India with him.

As he prepares to leave, St John spots something on Jane's sketch which makes him "dexterously tear a narrow slip from the margin". Jane has signed her real name, *Jane Eyre*, and this discovery by St John will lead to Jane's inheritance.

Chapter 33

The next day, St John returns to Jane's cottage. He has learned the details of Jane's past, and he now recites this to her at length – whether to watch her reaction or impress her with his memory skills, we do not know – without revealing at first that he knows who she really is; the information came in a letter sent by Mr Briggs, the solicitor (the same one who halted the wedding between Jane and Rochester). Now St John shows Jane the scrap of paper taken from her drawing, which clearly shows the signature of *Jane Eyre*. Jane ignores this at first and instead asks if he knows where to find Rochester. St John tells her that he has disappeared.

The solicitor's letter also brought the news that Jane's uncle, Mr John Eyre of Madeira, is dead, and his fortune has been bequeathed to Jane. She is rich! But she does not let herself get carried away: "we contain ourselves, and brood over our bliss with a solemn brow." There is also the burden of knowing that her only surviving relative is now deceased. However, Jane *has* inherited the magnificent sum of £20,000 (£2,000,000 in today's money, more or less). The thought of financial independence is "glorious" to her.

Jane asks how it was that Briggs came to write to St John, and he reveals that his middle name is "Eyre", and that they are related: his mother is Jane's father's sister. St John, Mary, and Diana are all Jane's cousins. "Glorious discovery to a lonely wretch!" Jane exclaims. She is exhilarated by the news and straightaway offers to split the inheritance amongst all of them.

St John does not at first think she is serious. Jane explains that "it is fully a matter of feeling as of conscience: I must indulge my feelings; I so seldom have had an opportunity of doing so." St John finds fault with her proposal, but Jane responds that she has always wanted a family. When St John tells her that she may yet marry, Jane replies: "Marry! I don't want to marry, and never shall marry." She ends by saying, characteristically: "No one would take me for love." The self-denigration is never more than a thought or two away (even though Rochester confessed that he *did* love her, which Jane could hardly have forgotten).

After some discussion, the Rivers agree to Jane's proposal, the matter is settled, and "St John, Diana, Mary, and I, each became possessed of a competency."

Chapter 34

ST JOHN MAKES HIS PROPOSAL

Christmas. Jane reflects benignly on her pupils (while dismissing the "ignorant, coarse, and besotted" peasants of Europe!). Jane irritates St John by telling him of her plans to make Moor House festive for Diana's and Mary's homecoming. St John diminishes any pleasurable anticipation on Jane's part by insisting that she contemplate more elevated matters: he refers to "common-place home pleasures" as "trite transient objects". For a restless, dissatisfied soul like St John's, there *is* no home except in the clouds with the angels – but a home (on firm ground) is all Jane has ever wanted. She abruptly cuts off his lecturing.

When Jane has painstakingly completed the preparations, St John shows no appreciation at all for her work. It appears that only quixotic pursuits – like becoming a missionary – can offer *him* pleasure (and isn't that a form of selfishness, to disparage the good-natured efforts of others?). Jane begins to cool on him: "he lived only to aspire", she thinks to herself; "he would never rest; nor approve of others resting round him", and "I comprehended all at once that he would hardly make a good husband: that it would be a trying thing to be his wife". (Bronte, with her customary ironic touch, is about to have St John propose marriage to Jane.) Nonetheless, Jane recognises and appreciates his lofty nature – and how appropriate a life as a missionary will be for him.

Diana and Mary arrive at the house. All is goodwill and glad tidings (but not for St John; it is something of a relief to him when he is called away to tend a sick parishioner). Later, he announces that he will leave England sometime within the next year.

St John discloses the news that Rosamond Oliver is engaged, and having announced this, according to Jane, he is "as serene as glass" about it. Jane notes that "his reserve was again frozen over, and my frankness congealed beneath it." He treats Jane differently from his sisters, with "little chilling differences" between them. "I felt the distance between us to be far greater than when he had known me only as the village schoolmistress." (Although he took the quarter-share of Jane's legacy, he cannot *bear* being in her debt – his pride won't allow it – and we never witness him thanking her even once for the £5,000, a lot of money in those days.)

Later, he cryptically tells Jane that "the battle is fought and the victory won" – except that the battle was *not* fought, Rosamond just gave up on him and found someone else! St John rejoices that "the event of the conflict is decisive: my way is now clear". It appears that Rosamond's impending marriage to another man has released him from any lingering affection towards her.

Jane notices that St John casts glances in her direction as she studies (he is sizing her up before his grand proposal to accompany him to India). He exhorts her continually to ignore tiredness, poor weather, and discomfort ("her constitution is both sound and elastic", he notes, uncharmingly). He tells her to give up German and study Hindustani. Jane finds she cannot resist his pressure and drives herself harder to impress him.

Jane remains in his thrall, the more so because he will not soften towards her; he seems to want one aspect of her only (the workhorse), while ignoring the rest of her personality – her creativity, her sensitivity, her need for camaraderie. The more St John tries to make Jane submit to his will (as he has submitted to God's), the harder she works to please him. She thinks to herself: "I, like a fool, never thought of resisting him – I could not resist him." Eventually, she breaks down in tears, but all St John says, is: "We will wait a few minutes, Jane, till you are more composed." (Unfeeling brute.)

Jane hankers for news of Rochester, but there is none; letters to Mrs Fairfax go unanswered.

One day, St John orders her out of the house to take a walk with him. Jane reflects on their relationship: "I know no medium: I never in my life have known any medium in my dealings with positive, hard characters, antagonistic to my own, between absolute submission and determined revolt. I have always faithfully observed the one, up to the very moment of bursting, sometimes with volcanic vehemence, into the other, and as neither present circumstances warranted, nor my present mood inclined me to mutiny, I observed careful obedience to St John's directions..." To sum up: watch out, St John.

After he and Jane have walked and found a place to rest, St John looks around him at the glorious panorama of scenery and says:

"And I shall see it again...in dreams, when I sleep by the Ganges; and again, in a more remote hour – when another slumber overcomes me – on the shore of a darker stream." In spite of his relative youth and his noble aspirations, St John appears to want nothing more than being joined to his God in an early death. We may ask what it is that makes a man want to abandon the real world and instead yoke himself to a fantasy, and the answer might well be: fear of living.

St John informs Jane that he will leave England in six weeks. He commences a lecture – sermon might be a better word – speaking of God's mastery over him, and the world's "feeble fellow-worms" (he appears to have little respect for his fellow man, a rather regrettable fault in a missionary). Then he turns his attention to Jane and begins his campaign to persuade her to accompany him to India. Jane's reaction is not what he would have wished for: "I was no apostle, – I could not behold the herald, – I could not receive the call."

Now St John makes his big move – and he is not clever about it. He tries to *order* her to marry him (which shows just how little he knows the real Jane, who longs for courtship and affection – and does *not* like being told what to do). "God and nature intended you for a missionary's wife", says St John. "A missionary's wife you must – shall be. You shall be mine: I claim you – not for my pleasure, but for my Sovereign's service." Jane ignores the bit about being his wife – too shocking to contemplate right then – and replies: "I am not fit for it: I have no vocation." St John, still thinking he has the advantage, and that he can browbeat Jane into agreement, tells Jane to have faith, to put her trust in God. Jane attempts to rebuff him. St John attacks again; he tells her he recognises "a soul that revelled in the flame and excitement of sacrifice." Yes, perhaps Jane does have a tendency to self-sacrifice (call it masochism), but what St John does not take into account, for all his highbrow intelligence, is that Jane has *already* sacrificed so much, suffered so much, in her life – she has no more desire for sacrifice and suffering. Now she wants to live *her* life, not St John's – not even God's. However, Jane feels herself surrendering to St John's persistent and powerful hold over her (coercion, we might call it). She asks for time to consider. St John is obliged to allow it.

She thinks about Rochester – gone forever. Why stay, then? Yet she knows that if she leaves England for India, she will work herself to her limits and beyond for St John, with the inevitable result of "premature death". However, the challenge tempts her; it is, after all, tempting to test oneself. But Jane already knows that she can never be his wife – there is no love on his side (and, although she does not admit it to herself right now, there is no love on *her* side, either, as she declared earlier in the chapter, when she said he would not make a good husband).

So Jane makes St John an offer: she is prepared to accompany him, but not to marry him. "I regard you as a brother – you, me as a sister: so let us continue." St John demurs. He *insists* they must be married – and the more he tries to reassure Jane that he does not want her as a woman but merely as a missionary's aide, the more she recoils. Jane *wants* to be a woman – and *married* – but only if there is love on both sides. '"Oh! I will give my heart to God," Jane says. "You do not want it."'

Jane is not afraid of St John, so she can do battle with him, just as she did all those years before with Mrs Reed; she "felt his imperfection, and took courage. I was with an equal – one with whom I might argue – one whom, if I saw good, I might resist."

St John now tries to use moral blackmail on Jane, suggesting that together and married, while their "Maker" looks down on them, they would function more effectively. But Jane has made up her mind. His *wife*? "Oh! It would never do!" she exclaims. As his companion, she could do anything required of her – "my heart and mind would be free. I should still have my unblighted self to turn to: my natural unenslaved feelings..." But as his wife, she would, she admits it, be his *slave*. Jane craves independence of mind and body, freedom of spirit and movement: complete autonomy. There is no way she will get that with St John.

Jane continues to provide reasons to herself for not marrying him: "There would be recesses in my mind which would be only mine, to which he never came; and sentiments growing there fresh and sheltered, which his austerity could never blight, nor his measured warrior-march trample down: but as his wife – at his side always, and always restrained, and always checked – forced to keep the fire of my nature continually low, to compel it to burn inwardly and never utter a cry, though the imprisoned flame consumed vital after vital – this would be unendurable." (How many tens of millions of women throughout history must have reasoned like this with themselves – and yet still married men who did, inevitably, deprive them of their life force, their energy and creativity, with their endless male demands.)

Again, she offers to go as a friend, but she will *not* marry. St John continues to insist that she *must* marry: it is the only way. Now Jane becomes incensed – the "mutiny" against oppression, of which she spoke earlier, erupts, and she blurts out: "I scorn your idea of love...I scorn the counterfeit sentiment you offer: yes, St John, and I scorn you when you offer it." Her inner fire blazes, just as it did when she spoke the truth to Mrs Reed a decade earlier. St John is surprised – shocked! – at these words, and he recoils (his pride is hurt, his huge ego is bruised). Jane asks him again to abandon his scheme of marriage. St John departs while issuing dire warnings, telling her to "tremble" in case she should be numbered amongst those "who have denied the faith and are worse than infidels!" His final, parting shot falls well wide of the mark. Jane ignores it. But she understands only too well "the disappointment of an austere and despotic nature" which has "met resistance where it expected submission"; "in short, as a man, he would have wished to coerce me into obedience..."

Jane is the first true feminist in literature, recognising the spurious male prerogative to subdue and obligate the female – and fighting back. And winning.

That night, St John exhibits his hurt - and his hitherto well-disguised weakness of character - by dismissing Jane peremptorily at bedtime. She asks for his forgiveness; he replies that he has nothing to forgive, "not having been offended." How little he knows himself, or wants to know himself: he has been cut to the very quick, and he will never forgive Jane for it.

"And with that answer he left me," she notes. "I would much rather he had knocked me down."

It is worth mentioning that this sequence, the argument over marriage and submission between St John and Jane, is executed over a lengthy eight pages; we may take it that, in its detail and density, the matter was of special interest to Charlotte Bronte and may even be a fictive version of a real conversation she had with a man.

Chapter 35

Until his departure a week later, St John makes Jane pay for rejecting him by being icily polite; he will never pardon her for the "scorn" she showed to his offer of marriage. Jane attributes no malice or desire for vengeance to him, but some might see in his refusal to accept another person's point of view a deep fault in his psyche. He certainly enjoys hurting Jane ("All this was torture to me", she thinks), although he would surely deny it - but he also enjoys hurting himself. He *likes* pain: the pain of refusing to understand other people, the pain of always maintaining his emotional distance, the pain of giving his heart and soul in the name of Faith to a religion which demands more and more of him, and the pain of rejecting marriage with a woman he loves in the name of self-denial.

Jane tries to traverse the gulf that has opened up between them, but St John is not interested in reconciliation - he wants only obedience. While Jane speaks, he again raises the topic of marriage, causing Jane severe anguish. She accuses him of "killing" her, which, far from making him relent and retreat, spurs him onto the attack, accusing her of using "violent, unfeminine, and untrue" words. He tells her she merits "severe reproof", that her words are "inexcusable", but he (being the supercilious male Christian that he is) will - yes! - *forgive* her. Jane sees that her attempt to find a way around his pride has resulted merely in inflating it. Again they chew over his offer to take her to India (this is like a pair of lovers who quarrel madly because they must find a way to part – it is desperate, it is unreasonable); then St John, in his anger and frustration, tries to say that she *already* gave her agreement to go. Jane is taken aback by this underhand manoeuvre. "Now I never had, as the reader knows, either given any formal promise, or entered into any engagement..."

They continue to argue about it. Jane tells him that she would "not live long in that climate", to which he claims she is "afraid", and Jane responds that "God did not give me my life to throw away..." No, indeed, for unlike Helen Burns and St John Rivers, those exemplary Christians, Jane is not absolutely convinced that life after death will be so much better than life here on earth – if indeed there *is* such an afterlife (which Jane herself has questioned). Finally, she tells him that she must discover Rochester's fate, and until she knows it, she can do nothing else. St John ends the conversation by dismissing her with "I had thought I recognised in you one of the chosen." More spite, and more misreading of Jane's character. She does not bow to threats.

Jane is obliged to explain to Diana the situation with St John. She tells his sister that she could not love him as a husband, and when Diana mentions that he is "a handsome fellow", Jane reverts to her former self-apology (or self-pity), replying curtly, "And I am so plain you see..." Jane continues her analysis of the proposed marriage union, explaining to Diana that "it is not himself, but his office he wishes to mate. He has told me I am formed for labour – not for love..." Jane envisages that what might well happen if she went to India with him as his wife would be a "torturing kind of love for him", and if he rejected that love, she would be "unspeakably wretched".

In the evening, St John reads from the *Book of Revelation* (the preferred section of the Bible for doomsayers and nihilists), reinforcing to himself "the greatness and goodness of his purpose", as Jane describes it, and again she is awed by him. Afterwards, he persists in his adjuration to Jane to follow him to India: "I cannot give you up to perdition as a vessel of wrath: repent – resolve; while there is still time." It is a threat, plain and simple: fail to follow God's order (St John's order), and you will regret it – perhaps eternally; he is implying that the future of Jane's very soul hangs in the balance. Jane is again swayed, moved, bent by his self-righteous power; she feels a "veneration" for him that almost overturns her resolve to back away, as she was almost persuaded the first time he "beset" her; but, in the end, "To have yielded then would have been an error of principle; to have yielded now would have been an error of judgment." St John's divinely infused power works on her, but, for all its force, "I knew all the time, if I yielded now, I should not the less be made to repent, some day, of my former rebellion. His nature was not changed by one hour of solemn prayer: it was only elevated." In other words, Jane understands all too well that he is a tyrant, given to seeking vengeance for supposed wrongs done to him in the past. Yet Jane has *still* not completely freed herself from his reach; she says that if only she was "convinced that it is God's will I should marry you, I could vow to marry you here and now – come afterwards what would!" St John, exclaiming in triumph, thinks he has overcome her resistance at last. Jane admits she is "excited more than I had ever been..." She is on the very edge of the abyss.

And then, while Jane experiences "an inexpressible feeling" (it is her powerful will, which has given her the strength to fight adversity all her life, beginning to give way), she hears a voice, a cry: '"Jane! Jane! Jane!" And she *knows* that voice – it is Rochester's. She responds: "I am coming!" She runs to the front door and opens it: "Where are you?" There is nothing; there is no reply. But she *heard* it; it is enough to convince Jane that she has received a sign.

This is the crucial moment in the story (the Greeks called it "peripeteia", an important change or turn). Why is hearing Rochester's voice so critical to Jane at the moment she is about to succumb to St John's pressure? Because it shows us that Jane is no longer under the direct command of God (or His agent, St John); rather, instead of the Deity, she chooses Man (in the form of Rochester). *The voice she hears in her head in that mystical, visionary moment is the stronger voice: and it is not God ordering her to follow St John, but Rochester pleading with her to go to him.* It is not that Jane suddenly *rejects* God – she doesn't – but simply that (unlike St John, who has abandoned mortal comforts) Jane wants to live a life like other people, ordinary people, experiencing both good and bad, for better or worse. Jane has always called on God in times of trouble (receiving in response the strength to leave Thornfield instead of becoming Rochester's mistress, for example), and, in the last paragraph of the book, which is given over to St John's appeal to be reunited with God in death, it is clear that Jane's allegiance to the Deity has not waned - but it is shared now with Rochester. This moment - Rochester's summons and the rejection of St John - can be seen as the triumph of Jane's life, the moment when she finds the mental strength to part forever from oppression and live for herself.

In her own words:

"I broke from St John; who had followed, and would have detained me. It was my time to assume ascendancy. My powers were in play, and in force. I told him to forbear question or remark; I desired him to leave me: I must, and would be alone. He obeyed at once. Where there is energy to command well enough, obedience never fails. I mounted to my chamber; locked myself in; fell on my knees; and prayed in my way - a different way to St John's, but effective in its fashion. I seemed to penetrate a Mighty Spirit; and my soul rushed out in gratitude at His feet. I rose from the thanksgiving - took a resolve - and lay down, unscared, enlightened - eager but for the daylight."

This extraordinary moment of revelation shows us the power of Jane's pristine visionary intellect, which can steer her onto the correct path even as she feels that another's influence is too great for her to resist. It is the difference between the cold discipline of St John and her own hot-blooded, fiery intensity: the fire melts the ice and burns supreme, a hard, gemlike flame that cannot be extinguished by any man.

Chapter 36

St John slips a message under Jane's door next day, June 1st. It is part threat ("enter not into temptation") and part peace offering ("the spirit...is willing, but the flesh is weak"); he persists in thinking his will can overcome hers and he refuses to acknowledge that he has been bested (by a woman, yet). The note asks for her "clear decision" later that day. Jane rejects any suggestion of weakness on her part and makes plans to leave for Thornfield and Rochester.

STAGE SIX: JANE'S RETURN TO THORNFIELD

Jane reflects on the "visitation" of the previous night (Rochester's voice in the air), and whether it was a "delusion" or an "inspiration"; she is sure it is the latter. The call has "opened the doors of the soul's cell, and loosed its bands…" She determines to find out in person what has happened to the man she loves. Jane, who has been with the Rivers for a year now, tells the sisters she will be going away.

It takes Jane 36 hours in the coach to reach her destination, and, having done so, she immediately sets off for Thornfield in a state of high excitement. "Could I but see him! - but a moment!" She approaches the mansion with great anticipation - and some trepidation. (Bronte builds the suspense by having Jane approach the house obliquely, via the orchard and meadow, so that neither Jane nor the reader sees what has happened to Thornfield before Jane is right upon it.)

When Jane arrives at an open and unobstructed view of Thornfield Hall, she looks up "with timorous joy"…and sees "a blackened ruin". The place "has the silence of death about it: the solitude of a lonesome wild." The building has been long abandoned, and Nature has taken possession of it.

Jane returns to the inn for answers (it's called "The Rochester Arms", and one wonders if Bronte named this ironically, given that Rochester has lost his hand!). The innkeeper tells her that the house was burned down – by Rochester's wife, Bertha. The keeper speaks of "a young lady, a governess" that Rochester "fell in -" (Jane interrupts him before he can use the word), and he adds that "nobody but him thought her so very handsome. She was a little small thing, they say, almost like a child." More of Jane's self-deprecation concerning her appearance, and we are used to it by now, but - there is something new here, a new kind of description: *almost like a child.* This warrants some further discussion, because it is the first time Bronte has used such an epithet on Jane.

Earlier, we discussed the image of the child, which crops up several times in Jane's dreams, and we have also discussed Jane's possible eating disorder;

however, this comment by the innkeeper introduces a new element concerning Jane's physique - it is, after all, the first time that Jane has actually been compared in size to a child. Why does it happen now? Because this sequence marks the most suspenseful moment in the story, the potential but uncertain reunion between Jane and Rochester, and Jane is at her most insecure, most apprehensive. When an unstable situation has arisen in the past, Jane has often begun to criticise herself; this time, having travelled on the coach for 36 hours in what must have been an advanced state of agitation (the hope of finding Rochester, the fear of having already lost him), she has eaten nothing. The hunger is overpowering, both for Rochester and for food, which she will deny herself until the situation is resolved. In Bronte's mind, Jane is no longer merely small - she is the size of a child. The intense pressure of Jane's feelings - the hunger of love, the love of hunger - have become commingled in the author's mind, producing this new epithet for Jane: the child.

"You see," the innkeeper continues, "when gentlemen of his age fall in love with girls, they are often like as not as if they were bewitched: well, he would marry her." We learn that when Rochester failed to find Jane after she had disappeared from Thornfield Hall, "he grew savage - quite savage on his disappointment: he never was a mild man, but he got dangerous after he lost her." Perhaps it is worth asking at this point just how different Rochester's "savageness" was after losing Jane - and Bertha's, after losing *him*? Is there one savageness for men and one for women? One *madness* for men and one for women? It appears so.

After Jane's disappearance, Rochester became like a ghost walking his own grounds, "as if he had lost his senses…" The innkeeper blames "…that midge of a governess…" (Bronte's continual obsession with Jane's physical appearance may well prompt the reader to speculate whose unkind voice it was in Bronte's head that obliged the author to project it onto her heroine - who, one wonders, used to deride *Bronte* so persistently for her apparent unattractiveness?)

The night of the conflagration, Jane is told, with Grace Poole drunk on gin, Bertha took the maid's keys, left her prison room, and set fire to the gallery wall hangings - and then Jane's former bed. Rochester saved all the servants, then went to find Bertha, who had gained access to the roof; she jumped before he could rescue her. If indeed he *did* try to rescue her.

Having saved everyone except Bertha, Rochester was felled by the collapse of the house around him as he made to leave, and, though rescued, "one eye was knocked out, and one hand so crushed that Mr Carter, the surgeon, had to amputate it directly. The other eye inflamed: he lost the sight of that also. He is now helpless, indeed - blind and a cripple." He lives at Ferndean, a farm he owns. Jane thinks: "I had dreaded worse. I had dreaded he was mad." (Mad like Bertha, perhaps? That would have been ironic, perhaps even justified, given Rochester's treatment of her.)

Jane asks to be taken directly to him.

Chapter 37

Jane arrives at an "ineligible and insalubrious site." It's a Gothic manor-house in a "gloomy wood". As Jane approaches, she sees Rochester at the door. He seems the same to Jane, except that he looks "desperate and brooding", like a caged animal. Jane is not frightened away. Indeed, she has "a soft hope...that soon I should dare to drop a kiss on that brow of rock..." His left arm, the mutilated one, he nurses. Everything is to him "void darkness", Jane notes. He stands in the rain until John the servant takes him back inside.

Jane knocks at the door and is given entry. The servant, Mary, is startled to see her. Jane asks her to tell Rochester that a person has come to visit him. This done, Jane enters Rochester's room with a tray. When she identifies herself to Rochester, he is overcome with joy. "My living Jane..." "My living darling!" He says that he "trusted that she would not leave me", to which Jane replies, "Which I never will, sir, from this day." Jane reveals that she is "independent" with "five thousand pounds".

Rochester does not believe she will stay, or that she will want to devote herself to a blind, lame person like himself. Jane tells him: "I am my own mistress." In other words, from now on, nobody tells me what to do. (This is another pivotal moment in the story: all her life, Jane has wanted financial independence and freedom from obligation.

Now she has both. Before, she was Rochester's governess, then the object of his desire: now she is his equal. On this footing, she is able to give herself to him freely.)

Jane offers to be of service in every way. She still hopes to be his wife, but at first he seems uncertain what their relationship will be. He enquires whether he should "entertain none but fatherly feelings" for her. She tells him she will be his nurse only, if that is what he wants. He says she will want to be married, and she replies: "I don't care about being married." We may take this to mean that she is prepared to be his nurse - and nurse only, not his mistress - if that is his choice. His sense of his own inadequacies (calling himself "a sightless block") returns him to despondency. Jane reassures him that his ruined arm, his blindness, only increase her love for him (because, of course, he is now completely in her power). They have supper together; she is "at perfect ease" with him, "because I knew I suited him". The couple fill each other with hope and joy.

Next day, on a walk together, Jane tells Rochester of her life since she left Thornfield. He complains about her leaving him, and he is jealous of St John. Jane reassures him. "All my heart is yours, sir: it belongs to you; and with you it would remain, were fate to exile the rest of me from your presence for ever."

"I am no better than the old lightning-struck chestnut-tree in Thornfield orchard…" he complains. Jane comforts him again and again. Rochester asks her to marry him, and she gives her assent. "To be your wife is, for me, to be as happy as I can be on earth." Rochester, seeking to reassure himself, asks her again how she feels about his infirmities. "I love you better now," Jane replies, "when I can really be useful to you, than I did in your state of proud independence, when you disdained every part but that of the giver and protector."

Rochester makes a heartfelt speech praising God's will and authority. He talks about a time a few days before when in despair during his prayers he called out her name - that was the moment she heard his voice in the air, but Jane does not disclose this. Rochester recognises God's hand in her return to him: "I thank my Maker, that in the midst of judgment he has remembered mercy. I humbly entreat my

Redeemer to give me strength to lead henceforth a purer life than I have done hitherto!"

Chapter 38

"Reader, I married him."

This famous line, delivered with such understatement, recalls the opening line of the book ("There was no possibility of taking a walk that day") in its simple artlessness. It is as if Jane has run out of violent emotion with regard to Rochester (and she has, after all, expended an awful lot of it since the time she first met him).

Rochester is supremely content as her husband; he tells Jane: "our honey-moon will shine our life-long: its beams will only fade over your grave or mine." He has even grown poetical in his happiness.

Jane closes her story with some information about the other characters:

St John writes infrequently, without mentioning Rochester or Jane's marriage to him.

Adele grows up, and "a sound English education corrected in a great measure her French defects." Jane discovers that Adele is, after all, "a pleasing and obliging companion".

We now learn from what vantage point Jane has been writing her story: she tells us that she has been married ten years, which makes her something in the region of 30 years old (she was 18 when she left Lowood and went to Thornfield, where she spent maybe half a year before leaving there after the wedding to Rochester was called off; she then went to live with the Rivers for a year before returning to Thornfield).

"I hold myself supremely blest – blest beyond what language can express…" she tells us, and that "I am my husband's life as fully as he is mine…No woman was ever nearer to her mate than I am…we are ever together." If more evidence of their devotion to each other was needed, she ends with: "All my confidence is bestowed on him, all his confidence is devoted to me; we are precisely suited in character - perfect concord is the result." (We might well ask if ever there *was* a marriage like this for its unblemished happiness, and, indeed, we should imagine that here was some wishful thinking on Charlotte Bronte's part for just such a kind of marriage.)

After two years of Jane's assiduous care, Rochester regains some sight in his remaining eye, and eventually all of it. They also have a child, a boy. "On that occasion," Jane reports, "he again, with a full heart, acknowledged that God had tempered judgment with mercy."

Diana and Mary are married to two good men, and, true to his mission, St John remains in India. He has not married. "His is the ambition of the high master-spirit", Jane adds. In his most recent letter to Jane, he seems to anticipate his own death and is well prepared for it. As he writes:

"My Master...has forewarned me. Daily he announces more distinctly, - 'Surely I come quickly!' and hourly I more eagerly respond, - 'Amen; even so come, Lord Jesus!'"

It is, perhaps, worth pondering why Bronte ends the book with an extract from St John's letter to Jane, rather than any final thoughts from Jane herself, and also why God has, so to speak, been given the pulpit for the final lines. It seems strange, somehow, but there must be a reason, and perhaps it is because Jane, in spite of transferring her allegiance from Deity to Man (from God to Rochester) during the course of the story, as we have earlier discussed, remains a steadfast Christian. God has, after all, been her guide and salvation during all the difficulties she has endured in her life. Her faith has comforted her, supported her, given her strength. So God has the last word.

Jane, too, one imagines, is prepared for death; she has a pure and unblemished conscience, having achieved everything she has ever desired in her life, while causing no suffering to others on the way. With Rochester by her side, with her trials and tribulations overcome (and with her complete independence, which was so important to her), we may well say that Jane Eyre has lived a good - indeed, the best - kind of life.

POSTSCRIPT (1)

Why does Rochester have to lose his sight and his hand?

If the ending of *Jane Eyre* is a happy one – and, on the surface, it seems to be, with Jane and Rochester reunited, plenty of money, and the blessing of a child – then why does Rochester have to suffer a double disability? (This would never have happened in your standard contemporary love story, it's too downbeat, too punitive.) Could Rochester not simply have failed to save Bertha when Thornfield was burning down and then escaped the collapsing building without such spectacular injuries? There is, of course, the matter of *karma*, or, if you prefer, God's Judgment: Rochester must suffer for his dissolute past life and his treatment of Bertha (if you subscribe to the notion that she was ill-treated, which many modern readers do), and the punishment is to deprive this formerly vigorous, athletic man's ability to function as he once did, by taking away his sight and his hand. In the sphere of cosmic comeuppance, Rochester's fate is no more or less unusual than similar fates to be found in Greek tragedy or Shakespeare, for example.

However, there may be another explanation, more complex, yet more specific, which springs from the text, although it is carefully concealed by the author. This explanation is somehow a lot more plausible than the workings of fate or the retribution of God.

During the course of the story, we have noted the many occasions when Jane turns in on herself, attacking her perceived unattractiveness, her personal background, etc. This self-deprecation happens so often in the story that it becomes a very noticeable motif, usually occurring when Jane is feeling vulnerable, oppressed, or apprehensive. (The author may very likely have shared these insecurities with her heroine.) To erase these feelings and ensure that they would not continue to bedevil Jane in the future beyond the end of the book – to give her heroine a truly happy ending – Bronte had to do something radical. The path the author chose was not to magically improve Jane's looks so that she becomes a beauty – Bronte would never have permitted such a travesty – but, rather, to ensure that Jane's great love, Rochester, would never be able to see her as he had seen her before: he had to lose his *sight* so that Jane's appearance becomes irrelevant. Beautiful or not, Jane would not have to worry about the matter again.

But doesn't he regain the sight in his remaining eye eventually? Yes, he does, but by then he is so dependent on Jane – and they have had, or are going to have a child, which binds them further together – that her looks are now immaterial to either of them.

Rochester's hand? He had to lose it for the sake of Jane's safety. Recall when Jane was trying to leave Thornfield after the revelation of Bertha's existence and the cancelled marriage: Rochester became furious with her refusal to accept his apologies and explanations, and he laid a hand on her to physically restrain her from escaping. Yes, he almost immediately removed his hand, while reasoning that even if he managed to prevent her *physical* departure, her *mind* would flee from him; Jane would shun and resent him. However, the damage had been done: Rochester had been physically abusive, and in order for this never to happen again, Bronte taught him a memorable lesson by removing his left hand. Rochester could not turn to violence a second time without being very aware of his disability, which would instantly check his actions.

In Bronte's mind, a maimed and partially sightless Rochester, henceforth relying on Jane to care for him, was rendered powerless. He would never be able to hurt her again in any way. Jane now had complete control.

POSTSCRIPT (2)

The singular power of the personal address

Charlotte Bronte wrote *Jane Eyre* using the first-person point of view for her eponymous heroine: the "I" pronoun. Her book is generally regarded as the original of this technique, a technique which has been taken up subsequently by thousands of authors who want to create an intimate relationship between their protagonist and their readers. Charlotte Bronte did it first, and she did it very well.

Jane speaks directly to the reader throughout the story, and such is the power and poetry of Jane's voice in our heads that we are held entirely captive. Jane never lets up in her close connection with the reader: we are carried along with her story, hoping for her, suffering for her, rejoicing for her, because her mind is so original and so complex, and what she says is so direct and compelling. Jane's unforgettable voice is the inspiration for a thousand literary heroines that were to follow her.

Jane does more than tell the reader what is happening in the story, what she is feeling and what she is thinking: she comes another step closer by directly addressing the reader on numerous occasions, advising us, informing us, warning us, appealing to us, over and over again, until we count Jane Eyre as a very close acquaintance, indeed.

The repetition of these personal addresses, the accumulation of these appeals to the reader, is very potent. The technique is one of the reasons that *Jane Eyre* still sells in large quantities, although set in a time so very different from our own. The mental connection created between Reader and Heroine bridges the almost 200-year gap between then and now with a single thought.

There are no less than 20 direct addresses to the reader (and there may be more):

1. "Let the reader add" Ch.5
2. "…and when I draw up the curtain this time, reader…" Ch.11
3. "While he is so occupied, I will tell you, reader, what they are…" Ch.13
4. "No, reader…" Ch.14
5. "No, reader, gratitude, and many associations, all pleasurable and genial, made his face the object I best liked to see…" Ch.15
6. "You are not to suppose, reader…" Ch.17
7. "I have told you, reader, that I had learnt to love Mr Rochester…" Ch.18
8. "Much, too, you will think, reader, to engender jealousy…" Ch.18
9. "Stay till he comes, reader; and, when I disclose my secret to him, you shall share the confidence." Ch.25
10. "Gentle reader, may you never feel what I then felt!" Ch. 27
11. "This is a gentle delineation, is it not, reader?" Ch.29
12. "…and yet, reader, to tell you all…" Ch.32
13. "It is a fine thing, reader, to be lifted in a moment from indigence to wealth…" Ch.33
14. "Perhaps you think I had forgotten Mr Rochester, reader, amidst these changes…" Ch.34
15. "Reader, do you know, as I do, what terror these cold people can put into the ice of their questions?" Ch.34
16. "Now I never had, as the reader knows, either given any formal promise, or entered into any engagement…" Ch.34
17. "Hear an illustration, reader." Ch.36
18. "And, reader, do you think I feared him in his blind ferocity?" Ch.37
19. "Reader, it was on Monday night – near midnight – that I too received the mysterious summons…" Ch.37
20. "Reader, I married him." Ch.38

Dear Student!

Thank you for buying this work.

I hope you have found it original, stimulating, and useful.

Please accept my best wishes for your coming exams.

Yours faithfully

Christopher Grey

Printed in Great Britain
by Amazon